Mind Games; Functional Seizures & Epilepsy: A Dual Diagnosis

By Linda McClure

Mind Games; Functional Seizures & Epilepsy: A Dual Diagnosis, Linda McClure

Copyright 2024 by Linda McClure. All rights reserved.

No part of this publication may be used without the prior written consent of the publisher.

Editor and cover design, Virginia O'Dine, Brilliant Fiction.

ISBN 978-1-7388198-3-6 **(Paperback edition)**

ISBN 978-1-7388198-4-3 **(Kindle edition)**

DEDICATION

Love ya, D!

For Kyle, the strongest person I know and admire.

To all who struggle, wishing for a normal existence.

To the doctors, researchers, and caregivers, whose support we appreciate.

And, to those with a dual diagnosis of epilepsy and functional seizures. Be kind to yourselves, take time for yourselves, and always remember, you're not alone.

Hugs,

In memory of Dr. Robert T. Fraser, Ph.D., CRC
Professor Neurology, Neurological Surgery, &
Rehabilitation Medicine University of Washington

There's a stillness within my mind, broken and exposed, disturbing the serenity.

Oh, the pain and suffering, pulling me down into insanity; in a space of no time.

I'm sucked into a vortex of chaos living in fear frantically searching for a release from its grasp.

There are no drugs to soothe the storms of my soul that imprisons my body and mind.

I'm slipping into oblivion engulfed by abysmal thoughts and unexpressed emotions.

ACKNOWLEDGEMENTS

They say it takes a village to raise a child and the same could be said for writing this book. Without my son, I wouldn't be here to finish it and I mean that literally. You're my tower of strength, my caregiver, my roommate, and best friend.

Virginia O'Dine, my fabulous editor who firmly, but gently, steers me in the right direction. I couldn't have published this or *Battles of The Mind* without your guidance. You're awesome!

To all the medical professionals here in Calgary, the US, and UK, I thank you for sharing your knowledge and expertise not only with epilepsy but of FND with seizures. Your devotion to your craft, to your patients, and research is commendable. I appreciate the time taken to answer my questions, to educate me, and support my effort in sharing my experiences.

Dr. Paolo Federico, Dr. Colin Josephson, Dr. Jessie Moorman, Dr. Sophie Macrodimitris, Dr. Ruby Sharma, and Dr. Samuel Wiebe. Epileptologists and neuropsychologists of Calgary, Alberta. Thank you for your support and sharing your collective wisdom and experience. I couldn't have gotten this far without your guidance and support for this worthwhile, and much needed, endeavour.

Thank you to Drs. Markus Reuber of the UK and Lorna Myers in the US for replying to my emails. I'm overwhelmed with gratitude that each of you replied to emails from this unknown individual from Canada.

This list wouldn't be complete without mentioning the Epilepsy Association of Calgary. So many generous souls have crossed my path and to each of you, thank you, you're all angels in my book and a blessing to all Albertans living with epilepsy and functional seizures.

To the counsellors and educators, Jennifer LaBelle and Taylor Riglin the insight, wisdom, and empathy you've exhibited is extraordinary. To the volunteers who've put in oodles of hours to aid in the programs offered by the association. Board of Directors, Gina Ross, Evan Legate, Ashley Anderson, Tasha Engel, Lisa Farstad, Grace Fung, Dr. Julia Jacobs-LeVan, Tyler Kilborn, Derek Payne, Dr. Andrea Salmon, Vicktoria Tulk, Harsh Vardhan, and Executive Director, Laura Dickson, thank you for your continued dedication to a worthwhile charity. We couldn't get by without you.

To my other best friend, Derek Payne, I count my blessings for having met you. You're an amazing person unlike any I've ever encountered. Don't ever change.

Hugs,

DISCLAIMER

I am not a medical professional and am not suggesting, prescribing, or offering medical advice. The words written within are comprised of my journal entries, poetry and social media posts, with references to reputable websites for the purpose of education and awareness.

Mind Games is the continuing story of my experiences with epilepsy and functional seizures. The average individual, and some medical professionals, have limited knowledge of FND² (functional neurological disorder) with or without seizures which I hope to change with this book.

My functional seizure diagnosis weeks after moving to Calgary followed by the global pandemic six months later, and the added feelings of isolation were tantamount to the challenges I faced over the next four years.

My personal experiences, the books, articles, and research findings I've read are strictly for informational purposes. Unlike Battles of The Mind, Mind Games is more than a memoir, it's a blend of reality and theory.

Some of the names have changed to respect privacy.

TABLE OF CONTENTS

DEDICATION 2
ACKNOWLEDGEMENTS 4
DISCLAIMER 6
INTRODUCTION 11
CHAPTER ONE 13
   Who Am I? 13
   I Have What?? 16
CHAPTER TWO 19
   What Are Functional Seizures?[1] 19
      Consider this… 19
   What is the difference?[2] 20
   How do functional seizures happen?[2] 20
   What symptoms or signs can happen during a functional seizure?[1]
.... 21
   How Common are functional seizures?[2] 24
   My Functional Seizures 25
CHAPTER THREE 29
   +*What is Trauma and its effect on epilepsy and FND*[2] *with seizures?*[4] 29
CHAPTER FOUR 33
   Only Believe In What You Can See & Half Of What You Read 33
CHAPTER FIVE 37
   Where's The Toggle Switch? 37
   If you can't see or touch it don't think it isn't real 37
   Mindfulness Techniques 39
   Talk Therapy 40

CHAPTER SIX 43
   Who Are We? 43
      What is Normal? 43
   Spring cleaning; rearranging the old 46
   and making it new again. 46
   Dem Walls 47

THE COVID YEARS—2020—2022 49

CHAPTER SEVEN 51
   2020 51
      A Pandemic—Death and Mourning 51
   Mom / Nana August 1933—April 2020 RIP 56

CHAPTER EIGHT 88
   2021 And The Shit Keeps Coming 88

CHAPTER NINE 134
   2022—Weights And Measures—A Balancing Act 134

CHAPTER TEN 159
   2023—New Possibilities 159

CHAPTER ELEVEN 177
   2024—Hope 177

SMU VISIT 2024 195
   JULY 11, 2024—JULY 18, 2024 195

FINAL THOUGHTS 207
   What we need is… 207

One Last Message 210

NOTE TO READER: 214

DEFINITIONS 218
   Project UPLIFT[7] 218

WEBSITES 223

RESOURCES 225

BIBLIOGRAPHY 231
  Functional Neurological Disorder—FND² 231
  Epilepsy 232
  Others 233
AWARENESS EXERCISE 234
EMOTION JOURNAL 235
ABOUT THE AUTHOR 236
WHAT DO I MEAN BY MINDFULNESS? 237

INTRODUCTION

It's funny how you get to know yourself when faced with a chronic illness. I know for me, that has certainly been the case. How I see myself now has altered since epilepsy and FND[2] with seizures entered onto the scene. Things that used to matter so much to the point of obsession are brushed aside. The compulsion to clean, organize, and control every aspect of my life isn't the same. "In the big scheme of things, does *this* really matter?" is a phrase I often use. Recalling my ex-mother-in-law's view of daily cleaning resurfaces often. Her belief that dusting is a futile chore, commenting "why bother to dust? When I die, I'll only create more." Her witty, warped humour and funny way of looking at life in an off-hand way was a constant source of amusement. But it did carry some truth to it. Life is too short to worry about the little things which cause so much angst. Wanting to keep up with the "Joneses", comparing ourselves to others, trying to fit into a mold we don't belong in. It's better to forge our way through as independent, unique souls, fearless in our beliefs and unafraid to stand up for them.

Reminding myself that regardless of my health conditions, of which there are many, the 'me' from ten years ago has changed. Going through challenges, dealing with outside stressors, and those within, experiencing sorrow, joy, pain, and all those anxious moments which paralyze us, can we get to know ourselves, the person we were born to be. The built-in characteristics are like the DNA of the soul. Isn't easy to accept, isn't difficult to say but is so hard to accomplish.

Acceptance is a willingness to adapt to changing circumstances. Realizing nothing remains the same forever. Acceptance is acknowledging there isn't a timeline or set process to how we progress through our journey since birth.

Adaptability isn't a weakness, not a sign of inferiority or manipulation. Adapting to situations takes strength and the ability to explore new ideas and ways of accomplishing routine activities or learning new concepts.

However, ignorance and stubbornly holding onto outdated, misconceived beliefs doesn't serve any purpose to those helping others seeking solace from health conditions they have no control over.

CHAPTER ONE

Who Am I?

I wasn't one to run to the doctor for every little thing, and rarely filled a prescription. But that all changed in the Spring of 2015 when, at forty-nine, I was diagnosed with epilepsy. An independent woman in the prime of her life suddenly flung into uncharted territory. My life was in chaos. I had no power. The inner strength I'd always relied on wasn't there. I'd always managed on my own, but adapting to this altered life was a challenge. Like most, I knew of epilepsy and assumed all seizures were alike, were all grandmal tonic-clonic events. But those were just one of over forty types. Many go unnoticed, come, and go as quick as a blink of an eye as a multitude of neurons burst, overloading the senses.

During those early days after my epilepsy diagnosis, when my world had spun out of control, I questioned everything. What is this disease? Will it go away? Will I ever be the same again?

Questions about the surgery and if my memories would remain intact, would I be me afterwards? What will my future hold? And so on. There was an inner turmoil within which I couldn't describe or understand myself, let alone put into words. And I wasn't alone. Those around me had similar questions. What they saw was a Linda who wasn't Linda. A crushed spirit no longer perky and positive. They didn't know how to deal with this new version, one so different from 'the old Linda'. We all struggled to adjust, but the hardest part, for me at least, was the well-intentioned comments of how I wasn't the same, but that after the surgery, I'd be back to my old self. Those periodic statements, meant to be encouraging, were only reminders of what I'd lost. It was difficult to hear. Depressing to know I'd morphed into a stranger to those closest to me. I looked like 'Linda', I sometimes sounded like 'Linda', laughed, and joked like her, but I wasn't 'Linda'.

Living with a chronic illness knowing there's no cure, where your life is turned upside down, inside out, and sideways is hard. It's disturbing to be unsure of who you are and where you fit into the here and now. It's a complicated adjustment, ongoing, never ending, and not just for me. We, the sufferers, so tuned into ourselves, and rightfully so, aren't aware of the effects on our loved ones. The devastation of body and mind is a group effort, unfortunately. The one with first-hand knowledge of the disease through experience and those around them left to watch, helpless and frustrated, knowing there's nothing they can do to stop it.

Epilepsy took away my job, my license to drive, the ability to function as I once did. After my last surgery, I can barely type. My left hand was almost useless. I get confused easily, often forgetting where I'm going and how to get there. Such an overwhelming sense of loss, feeling helpless and useless. Fifty-four isn't old and yet I can't help but feel like a child trudging behind my son, staying close to keep him in sight. I rely upon him for every little thing. Delegating chores when I'm too worn out. Feeling I let him down. No longer the strong one, I now cling to him. So much worry and pain live behind these green eyes it's no wonder I swept it under the rug, hidden from view. And somewhere along the way, I've become so tormented I've lost the ability to control what is happening to me.

My first seizure back in 2011, I now believe, was an emotional breakdown. We often don't realize we're stressed until the source is gone or a breakdown occurs. Moving in with the boyfriend, coping with teenaged drama, holding down a stressful high-pressure job, created the right mixture. But my second seizure was different. I'd left that relationship the year before, had just returned from Disneyland when the volcano exploded. Call it a delayed reaction, a weak moment, whatever. The stressor eliminated, life was sorting itself out, and then all hell broke loose.

March 15, 2015, I almost died. My second seizure blew out the neurons, nearly suffocating me. My brain couldn't breathe, the oxygen depleting rapidly. That event opened a doorway to a new world, one fraught with trauma, stress, pain, and anxiety, like I never faced before. It swept me into another dimension, one where my bricks and mortar didn't exist.

Was the first one a functional seizure? Maybe. Epilepsy undoubtedly caused the second. Were both the result of stress and pent-up emotions, too much alcohol and poor eating and sleeping habits? Yes, I think they were. The epilepsy? We don't know why it suddenly started, gained traction, and sped off at the speed of light. We have no answers. Regardless, for me, the causes are the same. The treatment was different. The seizures are both long and debilitating.

As a person who suffers from both epilepsy and FND² with seizures, I'm susceptible to bouts of depression and anxiety. The triggers for each are different, as are their effects on my brain. Typically, most epileptic seizures are short, and caused by misfiring neurons that may or may not have a specific area of focus. They can occur in one part of the brain or spread all over. Medications or various surgical procedures may control them but, unfortunately, for some, like me, they're not controlled at all. The emotional effects are long lasting. Sadness, hopelessness, helplessness, frustration, fear, and sometimes anger. You want to isolate yourself, eliminate exercising to avoid injury. Many times, closing off contact with those able to support you. As with myself, some may have difficulty identifying what they're feeling and can't verbally express those emotions to themselves or others. Just like those with Alexithymia who have problems identifying emotions within themselves, have trouble in either detecting the emotions or even naming them. An issue I've experienced for most of my life.

I Have What??

I first heard of FND² with seizures in November 2017 but wasn't diagnosed until September 2019. When they discharged me from Calgary's Foothills Medical Centre, I returned to BC with instructions to seek therapy. I needed one-on-one therapy with a neuropsychologist, one familiar with functional seizures. But there wasn't such a creature back then in BC. After failing to locate a therapist, my doctors determined I could go without. The frequency wasn't often, and they felt it was manageable. We could revisit the situation should they increase in the future.

Looking in the rearview mirror, as I often do now, I wonder if we were wrong. What if we found a therapist who could have helped me? What if I developed the skills back then that I have today? Would it have made any difference? I'll never know. The past is behind me and I can not change it. I think I would have moved regardless of what occurred. Despite the functional seizure diagnosis, I hadn't any access to resources to treat my epilepsy. And Foothills was the only place I felt safe. I had faith in the doctors, nurses, and technologists got to know them and considered them my family. But even with their knowledge, they didn't know what it was like to have a seizure. Any seizure. They knew the science and latest procedures and that was it. They could understand the mechanics, but not how it felt. And despite the comfort of the surroundings, I was still lonely.

> *"When Linda wakes up in emergency, she doesn't know which seizure she's had."*
> *"It's difficult to tell which type Linda's had."*
> *"Your Dilantin levels are low. Did you miss taking your medication?"*
> *"What type of seizure did you have?"*
> *"We should increase your medication."*
> *"Yes. My Dilantin levels are low. They've always been."*
> *"No. Dr. Young does not want my medication increased. He doesn't, we don't, want me to become toxic again like back in 2018."*

With each trip to the emergency, I hope the seizure was an epileptic one, preferring the cause to be a physical manifestation not an emotional one. Even after all the therapy and books I've read, I still refuse to believe my emotional state is what drives the attacks. I felt guilty for wasting everyone's time, ashamed and mad at myself over the inability to control my emotions, ignoring how I feel and unable to manage my stress and depression. I feel useless and a burden frightened of the demon inside that controls me.

"You're a mystery Linda, an enigma. Your epilepsy is complex. Your epilepsy is showing signs of being progressive."
"The mind can only handle so much. Sometimes there are things happening inside that you're not even aware of."
"It isn't your fault."

And it isn't my fault. Blaming myself is unrealistic, and I need to be kinder towards myself. It's a functional neurological disorder and it's how my brain copes with trauma.

It's a lonely existence, an exhausting fight to justify the validity of your condition and how it affects all aspects of daily life. The empathy of those around you only goes so far and begins to wane when the episodes won't subside.

CHAPTER TWO

What Are Functional Seizures?[1]

Consider this...

Think of functional seizures as the rush of water when the flood gates open, engulfing all within its reach, branching out, shifting in and around obstacles as its power is unleashed.

Now, view this as a person whose stress has escalated to the point of bursting. A body and mind already traumatized, unable to manage the onslaught. It may be a repeat of some horrific deed or triggered by current events. Part(s) of the brain shut down, the software overloaded. The operating system remains active, whereas the technology required to perform more basic tasks has malfunctioned. Once normal functions have recovered and the system rebooted, the brain is operational again. But like a cyclist pedaling up a steep hill, progress is slow and requires effort. Stopping and starting, and the need to rest is a necessity to restore energy and resume normal bodily functions. Muscles sore and a mind still recovering from the onslaught of emotion can take days to recover sometimes more. And just as with life, the circle is complete until the next storm.

In other words, functional seizures are a response to stimuli without conscious awareness. Much like veterans or first responders triggered by sounds or senseless acts of violence. Traumatic events such as 9/11, Tsunamis, Hurricanes, and Tornadoes which stirs painful memories of death and destruction.

What is the difference?[2]

An **epileptic seizure** is a sudden, involuntary, and usually short change in behaviour, movement, sensation, and/or consciousness associated to an abnormal electrical pattern in the brain which is usually seen, but not always, at the time of the seizure in an EEG (electro-encephalogram).

A **functional seizure** is an episode or event that may look and feel similar to an epileptic seizure, but without the abnormal electrical changes. This means that while a functional seizure might look like an epileptic seizure, you would see none of the abnormal electrical activity as seen in epilepsy.

How do functional seizures happen?[2]

The process of retrieval and exchange of information in the brain becomes disrupted, causing a breakdown in how it disseminates the data. The Central Nervous System forms part of the information processing system and, just as software may experience glitches, so too can the brain's operating system, which can lead to symptoms of functional seizures.

The brain is a complex network of about eighty billion nerve cells which enables us to process massive volumes of information. When accurate handling of this information creates communication problems, a glitch occurs and how the brain sends or receives information becomes disrupted. When this happens, the brain reprograms itself over time, altering how automatic processes operate.

Simply put, these are seizures triggered by psychological trauma or stress that interrupt the regular flow of processes, inhibiting the body's ability to respond.

What symptoms or signs can happen during a functional seizure?[1]

Episodes can vary from person to person and in how they present. Therefore, there is no one indicator of a functional seizure. Some common symptoms or signs may or may not be present and exhibiting one or more of these does not confirm an event.

For example, my 'warning signal' for the functional seizures is quite like my epileptic ones. The 'rising' sensation is more like a vertigo effect or from standing up too fast. Your equilibrium is off balance causing a dizzy-like reaction. Many of the patients I've seen in the seizure unit have experienced the same effect with slight variations. Some may collapse as if they've fainted while others feel a sensation opposite to mine. Instead of a 'rising' sensation from the gut upwards, theirs start at the head and move downwards. Even the length of time and speed at which it moves can vary from person to person.

During my volunteer visits in the seizure monitoring unit (SMU), patients shared their experiences as witnessed by those close to them. "My partner says I'll be acting all normal like and then suddenly fall. I've hit my head, bruised both arms, and knees and have no memory of doing so." Another patient describes rubbing their thumb over the tips of the fingers on both hands. A slow repetitious movement like a grasshopper making music with its wings. And others in their sleep will move their legs around as if suffering from restless leg syndrome.

I've experienced left side weakness with my epileptic seizures and, to some extent, the functional ones. However, my functional seizures will also include paralysis, shaking, and the inability to speak. Of course, there is no telltale sign that differentiates between functional and epileptic seizures; but, some movements do suggest more of a functional event than epileptic. For example, pelvic forward thrusting.

In both cases, I've been fully aware of my surroundings and I've lost awareness, although, more often with an epileptic seizure than a functional. In the early days after my epilepsy diagnosis, I would have auras whereby I could see, hear, and talk during the episode. These only lasted a few moments whereas when I did lose awareness they could last an hour or more. Most recently, the functional seizures include tonic-clonic type movements and awareness of my surroundings, however, when at rest, I can't lift myself up.

Patients are sometimes completely mute during the episode, but have also cried, screamed, growled, exhibited gasping sounds, shouting, swearing, and uttering unrecognizable words.

During one of my visits to the SMU, I heard a patient cry followed by grunting as they began seizing. According to my son Devon, I've uttered the odd sound like moaning during some of my events.

Losing control of your bladder is the most embarrassing symptom and is one of the main reasons for not going out. Patients who've had this happen would rather stay home than endure a repeat performance. And I can relate. Four months prior to my first surgery I peed all over myself while sitting on patio furniture in Home Depot. I hadn't been aware of it until afterwards and was horrified, refusing to return to the store until months later.

On average, functional seizures are typically longer than epileptic seizures and can vary substantially. For example, my recent events persisted despite the Ativan for thirty minutes, while many I've met in the SMU have experienced seizures for as long as an hour, sometimes two.

Some doctors think patients bounce back quicker after a functional seizure than with an epileptic seizure and yet, some patients have taken hours, even a full day, to recover. Aftereffects may range from tiredness and the need to nap to a sense of relief and calm.

In conversation with patients and others I've met through the Epilepsy Association of Calgary, we all agree, recovery from our functional seizures isn't as simple as catching one's breath. Depending on the severity and length of seizure, it generally takes us five to seven days to return to pre-seizure status.

How Common are functional seizures?[2]

According to some studies, functional seizures account for about 15% of presentations to neurology clinics and is almost as common as migraines and some more common than MS and Parkinson's Disease. An interesting article from a recent study[3] of U.S. veterans found that those with a functional neurological disorder had a higher incidence of mood disorders, anxiety disorder, or post-traumatic stress disorder than those with epilepsy.

Living with any seizure disorder is challenging. There's the condition itself you must adjust to, the randomness, the fear before, during and after. Those closest to you don't understand, sometimes thinking you're causing them or lost your mind. There is so little research into how, why, and when this disorder arises. Why, individuals with similar situations of trauma and emotional issues may develop functional seizures and others don't.

The differences between them and epilepsy are so subtle that detecting them poses a challenge even for doctors specialized in functional neurological disorders. Only a visit to a seizure monitoring unit with electrodes pasted to the scalp and monitored on video 24/7 can doctors provide a proper diagnosis. So, if the professionals can't diagnose my FND[2] with seizures without these diagnostic tools, how then could I be sure?

Disconnected—disjointed—out of sync words scream inside my head, get stuck with no way out. Arms and legs paralyzed—no response—dormant refusing to listen. Panic and fear lay within my body explosive yet, numb, as if I died.

My Functional Seizures

The seizures come from an accumulation of stress over time and through repetition, I've developed a behavioural reaction to how my brain processes emotions, distress, or discomfort. It is quite possible I do not realize I'm emotionally stressed and may not recall a particular situation which preceded the seizure. In those cases, I'd detach myself from the physical and emotional experiences, and learned to associate these emotions as a threat. The anxiety over when and how bad the next event will be lowers my seizure threshold. Whether it's the neurons bursting or the brain itself that's become befuddled, an inner disturbance overflows consuming my outer shell. Right from the start, my epileptic seizures have been exceptionally long. So long, in fact, the chances of brain damage or death were a real possibility. I've lost awareness, lost control of both bladder and bowels, and bitten my tongue. In the earlier days, I would experience horrible smells, dizziness, and a rising sensation resembling panic or fear. But without a visit to the monitoring unit for video EEG monitoring, we couldn't have known for sure. I've met very few like me, others also affected by the physical strain, self-blame, embarrassment, and guilt regardless of seizure type. Heightened emotions overshadowing the ability to think rationally and perform basic functions. Constantly changing from operational to incapacitated requires an inner strength most cannot appreciate. Drained of all energy and a mind overcome by intense emotions is just as exhausting as any epileptic seizure I've experienced. Most times, my functional seizures include twitching, slurred speech, and light-headedness. I'm usually aware but often unable to respond and may lose awareness.

I've fallen out of chairs, bumped into walls and doors, and hit my head on the bathtub. I've twitched and jerked, rubbing my arm raw, repeatedly whacking arms, legs, and head on the floor. I've awakened in hospital, muscles sore, skin bruised, and barely able to move. It takes me a week, sometimes more, before I'm up and running, not quite at 100%. The pain is real, the seizures not a put on. I'm not looking for attention or drugs. I just want them to stop.

And although I received my diagnosis four years ago, I will occasionally ask myself what I did wrong? Why can't I stop it? Living with both functional and epileptic seizures is hard. My epilepsy is complex, always has been, the seizures long and present themselves in a multitude of ways. I've been told I've exhibited three or four different seizure types while in the (SMU) and my functional seizures being similar makes it difficult to ascertain which type I've had. Even now I feel guilty over the ambulance rides and hospital visits, as if I do not deserve the care or attention. Which is ridiculous. If there's no way we can know which type of seizure occurred and it hasn't stopped, of course it makes sense to call 911. If it were an epileptic seizure, I could suffer brain damage or worse. Do I want to die? No. Then, not all trips to the hospital *aren't* a waste of time and money, and I am *not* to blame. And if there's one thing I've learned these last nine years, is no one's health comes with a guarantee. Life has its own agenda, and no matter how hard we want to control it, we can't.

Whether it's epilepsy or functional seizures, the lack of resources, government funding, and public awareness, forces us to fend for ourselves. And it's the same for our families who struggle to understand, often feeling inadequate; the stress, and anxiety wearing them down. Caregiver burnout, they call it. Yes, there are a few support groups for those caring for loved ones with a functional neurological disorder but there isn't much available. I couldn't imagine what my son goes through each time I have a seizure. The inability to know the difference. Whether to administer Ativan or call 911. The sense of helplessness must be immense. I know it would be for me.

An epilepsy diagnosis at any age alters the path you travel, taking you to destinations you didn't know existed. It's a lonely existence yet affects many others. The parents who cannot heal their child, siblings helpless to understand and defend their sibling from their illness. Friends who cannot handle seeing their besties change before their eyes becoming someone they no longer recognize. And the treatments that don't work frustrate the medical professionals. As lonely as epilepsy can be, as difficult it is to manage the seizures, anxiety, and depression, I know there are others out there with both conditions like me. A community of warriors fighting an endless battle, hoping a magic cure will make it all go away. To be normal again.

CHAPTER THREE

What is Trauma and its effect on epilepsy and FND[2] with seizures?[4]

Trauma is "an emotional response to a disturbing event or situation that compromises one's sense of security." Traumatic events may occur over brief periods or years. Society views traumatic events in the extreme, from war veterans, plane or car crash victims. There's no doubt in my mind these events whether one-off or chronic negatively impact survivors and witnesses alike. But trauma includes more than wars, bigotry, and abuse, and can encompass a lifetime of chronic episodes.

An emotional disturbance of unsettling gases weighted by the unknown sliding topsy turvy equilibrium disturbed by an awakening. Blood halted by veins thickened by tension; breathing slows gasping unsteadily—suffocating. Limbs flailing unseeing barely holding on. as the drape closes swallowed by black.

A traumatic event can make it difficult to stay calm. For example, the anxiety of having a seizure and not knowing which one will occur. Those emotional triggers feed off each other becoming an ongoing cycle of waiting, anxiety, and depression. Our reaction to trauma is normal and shouldn't be viewed as 'there's something wrong with us and is a natural form of protection. We're programmed to avoid any danger which jeopardizes our survival. When we ignore those emotions, the pile of shit becomes unmanageable, and at some point, they will resurface and present themselves in other ways. Avoiding stress is often difficult. It's one thing to say it but another matter to avoid it.

Markus Reuber and Lorna Myers, two doctors specialized in their fields of medicine, are, in my opinion, the best resource for research and understanding the patient's experience. Below are their views on emotional stress and how it correlates with FND[2].

Markus Reuber,[5] professor of clinical neurology at the University of Sheffield, UK, describes FND[2] as a learned reaction the brain uses to avoid distress.

Lorna Myers,[6] psychologist and director of the Northeast Regional Epilepsy Group's psychogenic non-epileptic seizure program in New York City believes this reoccurring reaction becomes a normal response to anything distressing.

Think of the chronically ill who fight a losing battle against a medical condition and unable to remove its hold on them both physically and mentally. The ongoing effects of which there's no end in sight, is traumatic. I've encountered patients struggling with MS, Autism, PTSD, depression, anxiety, and, of course, uncontrolled epilepsy and FND[2] with seizures are exposed to trauma daily.

Both male and female patients fighting their battle with little to no support from loved ones.

The twenty-something whose parents are too busy at work or won't drive the twenty minutes to visit them.

A single mother of a six year old whose father believes she's faking her seizures, and her epilepsy isn't real.

And a fifty-five year old suffering from PTSD so intense, their therapist cajoled them into visiting the monitoring unit on the condition they could leave if it became too much.

The sudden onset of my epilepsy. The three years spent commuting to Alberta and the surgeries that hadn't produced the outcome we hoped for resulting in my move to Calgary. I was stuck in a fight-or-flight scenario of which I hadn't any control and its overwhelming effects on mind and body. My independence was gone as was the life I had before. All the stress, emotional upheaval, the decision to leave my beloved coast left scars which will never heal.

Traumatic events aren't particular to recent events. They can go back as far as early childhood, such as with the sexual assault I experienced as a child. I assumed I was to blame and suppressed the memory and moved on. Soon after my seizure diagnoses, the late onset with no treatment readily available brought back those memories and my penchant to push down and suffocate my emotional responses. Just like my walls when all the suppressed feelings burst out. The natural progression of event—suppress—stress—overflow—seizure is how I've dealt with trauma and overly stressful situations.

CHAPTER FOUR

Only Believe In What You Can See & Half Of What You Read

There is so much in this world we can't see and yet we know it exists. The wind. A tree falling in a forest. Oxygen. Carbon monoxide and a plethora of other gases. But we accept them, believe in their existence, and know they're real. Neurological disorders fall within that category, or some do. ALS, Alzheimer's, MS, and Parkinson's are real, even to those uneducated in them. Epilepsy falls into that same pile. Each of these has treatment plans, drug therapies and sometimes surgical measures. There's a science behind them, a measurable means of diagnosis.

There are no standard tests for FND[2] with seizures. No bloodwork, x-ray, CT or MRI scan to diagnose them and the only course of treatment is therapy, and, sometimes, prescription medications to treat anxiety, depression, or pain. All a by-product of the underlying disorder.

I've met and read about other patients who were told their seizures weren't real, that they were producing them, or were schizophrenic and crazy. Those comments weren't helpful and only made them feel ashamed and question their sanity. The instances of patients wanting nothing more than someone to believe them, would rather have epilepsy than a functional neurological disorder. I, too, have felt the same, hoping the seizure was caused by my epilepsy, an illness that was visual and could be cut out. With epilepsy, there are medications and various surgical treatments, some more invasive than others, which clearly shows whether they're working or need adjustment. With FND[2] with seizures, therapy is the only valid option. There aren't any medications, no miracle pills, or surgical procedures to fix the software problem. And there's no gauge to measure your progress. You can't see 'inside' your head, you can't see your thoughts or emotions and the effect they have on your brain. It's not like a broken bone you can x-ray and see it has mended.

People with epilepsy and those with functional seizures are subject to depression and anxiety. Stress is a trigger for both my epilepsy and functional seizures, with one often feeding off the other. The trauma from each event, the seizures themselves, trips to the emergency, body flooded with drugs, and sore from the seizure and ministrations of EMTs and ER staff is exhausting, physically debilitating, and depressing. It's easy to understand why people living with either condition have a higher risk of suicide than the general population. I've been on antidepressants since October 2016, and despite changes in dosages and medication, I still experience bouts of low moods and anxiety.

There's the stigma of having seizures, plus the outdated beliefs of having a mental health condition. Locating health care professionals who are familiar with them is limited, their exposure and level of understanding just isn't there, and the public knows even less. Those of us with both are faced with similar challenges, however, with a dual diagnosis, the incidents of seizures being mistaken as epileptic when in fact they're not, presents a complete set of different issues.

I feel like a dot, a small speck in the vast world of humanity dumped in the middle of nowhere. I feel small and insignificant, of no value in a world gone mad. I feel lost, tired of a society filled with hate, ignorance, and bias. I feel small within a circle of others, broken, unsure if I'll ever be normal; unable to take charge of the future, and create my own destiny.

My epilepsy isn't controlled, and my functional seizures are a work in progress. The lengthy duration of my epileptic seizures is what most experts consider a functional seizure to be. The similarities of the two is a doctor's nightmare. There's no one definitive characteristic to point to and say, 'that's a 'functional seizure' or 'it was an 'epileptic seizure'. My trips to emergencies have normally been considered epileptic in nature, to start with, sometimes changing to a functional seizure determination. Even so, without the aid of a video EEG, there's no proof either way. It's merely guesswork.

So, in essence, I have two seizure disorders which are not fully controlled. One can kill me, the other not, for the most part. There's hope for the one which doesn't have a vendetta against me; hope that one day it will go into remission and stay there. However, it's the other one, the one on a mission to consume me lurking in the background for any opportunity to strike. Not until a new drug is created, or a new surgical procedure approved, I will continue to have seizures, and pray they don't kill me.

CHAPTER FIVE

Where's The Toggle Switch?

There is no on-off switch for a functional seizure, no alarms or warning sounds like there is on a car dashboard. To find an effective treatment requires a clear understanding of what's going on and how best to fix it. Each person's triggers are different, their reasons for their FND² diagnosis and how long it took to figure out.

If you can't see or touch it don't think it isn't real

Many people with FND² are accused of faking their seizures. Sometimes those closest to them, such as family members and friends, will believe the seizures are a put on designed to gain attention. Often, it's medical professionals, those with little to no experience with FND² who accuse the patient of lying believing they can control their seizures. Their ignorance and misunderstanding can lead to anger, frustration, and can delay treatment. Fortunately, for me, my team of professionals are educated and experienced in treating FND². It was two years from when we first discussed the possibility of FND² to when I was diagnosed and started treatment. Far less than the seven-to-ten-year average by a long shot.

There was two years between the first discussion and when I received my diagnosis. Plenty of time to absorb the concept of FND[2] with seizures, and oodles of time to research, ask questions, and seek out therapy before the proverbial shoe dropped. But did it really make a difference? Did knowing there was a possibility make it any easier for me to accept the diagnosis? I don't think so. Granted, my case is somewhat unique, complicated in so many ways. If I hadn't experienced the trauma of multiple surgeries, drug toxicity, commuting, and ultimately moving to Alberta, COVID, and the ongoing seizures, maybe it would have been easier to accept. Unfortunately, the path I travelled from November 2017 to September 2019 wasn't all rosy and when the hammer fell, I was a deer in headlights, stunned, frozen in time, unable, and unwilling, to accept I was causing the seizures. Or at least that's what I told myself.

My treatment involved talk therapy (Cognitive Behaviour Therapy, aka CBT) which centred on stress reduction and being mindful of how my body reacts to emotions. The goal is to learn the skills to change my negative thoughts and behaviours and focus on each emotion or event realistically so as not to fall into the vicious cycle of anxiety and depression. I found this extremely helpful when my mind would go from zero to sixty assuming the worst case scenario, thereby raising my anxiety levels through the roof. By slowing down, breathing deeply and asking myself 'in the big scheme of things, does this really matter?' Through these reality checks I can think clearly and base my decisions on actuality versus assumptions.

Mindfulness Techniques

Since childhood, I hadn't learned to connect my physical feelings with my emotions often assuming my thoughts represented how I felt. Practicing mindfulness has helped me immensely since learning them back in 2020 when Dr. Samson and I started UPLIFT[7] here in Calgary. Taking time out to "listen" to what my body is saying, to "feel" what it is doing in any given moment, is a powerful tool.

As a society, we're often burning the candle at both ends, forcing ourselves to do more, go faster, be more efficient which only serves to increase our anxieties, highlight our shortcomings, and place inordinate amounts of pressure on ourselves and loved ones. To sit back, relax, and breathe turning our focus inwards is beneficial. Taking the time to notice the tension in our neck and shoulders, clenched teeth and hands, tensed muscles prepared for flight, informs us how stressed and out of sync we are with our bodies. Learning to relax, take naps when tired, or just closing our eyes to rest them, will make a huge difference to how we think and feel.

Of course, I'm not an expert, but I do have lived experience, read research articles and publications from reputable sources, and books, spoken with neurologists, neuropsychologists, and patients. Patients accused of faking their seizures feel guilty for the strain they've placed on family, caregivers, and medical services. It is a lonely existence, isolating, frustrating, and often an intense feeling of helplessness that no one should have to deal with.

For many there's a need, almost an obsession, to do more. To be all things to everyone. A misguided perception so deeply felt that we must do better, accomplish more, and overcome our seizures. The depression is real. The inability to stop the inner turmoil causing the seizures, to get control of our emotions and how they present themselves, is all-consuming, adding vitriol to an already explosive situation.

We're experts on isolation and avoidance sidestepping questions and the misconceptions of others who believe we're crazy. And yet, we're our own worst enemy. We just can't let go of who we were before. Can't foresee a positive or fulfilling future worth living. Feeling worthless and a burden incapable of functioning. And so many circumnavigate those troubled waters utterly alone. Having no family support or strong friendships to aid them along their journey.

Talk Therapy

I believe when most people think about 'therapy' lying on a couch in a doctor's office, therapist sitting in a chair with pad and pen, is what usually comes to mind. That stereotypical viewpoint isn't too far off, minus the couch maybe. Talk therapy is designed to help patients to identify any underlying emotional conflicts that may cause their seizures. The thought process here is expressing the conflicting emotions more effectively, the seizures are less prone to occur.

Talk therapy is where my treatment started. One-hour visits over a predetermined period is how we addressed the inner turmoil trapped inside me. It's surprising what comes out when you sit down with a specialist trained in FND² therapy. As Dr. Young stated after my diagnosis, 'sometimes things are going on inside that you're not even aware of'; he was right. Who knew the sexual abuse from my childhood had been lurking in the background, how my negative interactions with the opposite gender affected me. Compounded by an epilepsy diagnosis, the surgeries, moving, loss of parent, and COVID were all participating factors which led to the FND² diagnosis in September 2019. Talking to an unbiased professional whose only goal is to help you is a liberating experience. If it weren't for Dr. Harper, I never would have told my family about the sexual abuse. If it weren't for Dr. Harper, I wouldn't have sought out and read all the books on FND²; wouldn't have started this book.

There weren't any lying on couches, or stodgy old therapist sitting in a chair with pen and paper, my sessions took place in a regular office sitting in a chair with Dr. Harper relaxing at her desk. As far as doctor appointments go, it was a pleasant interlude where I could open the drawbridge allowing her inside my fortress. These sessions were the foundation I needed to gain control over the seizures. And it was Dr. Samson and UPLIFT[7] which tied it altogether.

Fortunately, my therapy commenced in November 2019 and several sessions were conducted prior to the COVID shutdown in March 2020. While in person appointments are preferred, the remainder of my sessions were on Zoom which provided ongoing support during the early days of COVID and the death of my mother on April 1, 2020. During that first year, my seizure activity rose exponentially increasing in frequency to every other week on average. It took until the spring of 2022 before they started to reduce. During that period from 2019 to 2022, we felt most of my seizures were functional rather than epilepsy but in 2023, we believe the tide shifted somewhat.

As my control over the FND² improved, probable indicators of epileptic seizures increased. In 2023, there were four seizures where 911 was called; half of them we believe were epileptic. Whether the decrease in my Dilantin had precipitated the increase, or possibly the FND² was in remission which made the identification of seizure type easier, is hard to say.

I'm split in two, an innie an outie and lost somewhere in between. By outward appearances, I embrace the world, caring and supportive. A believer of laughter is the best medicine and the power of positive thought. But the innie in me, is a different breed living in dark versus the light. The innie of my nature, is quiet keeping to herself. Happier alone, insulated from life lost in a world of her making. This inner being ponders a life of tragedy loss and grief. On a mission for answers and explanations to complex and irrational behaviours without scientific reason. This other self is depressed grieving for things now gone and not likely to come back. And yet, despite the turbulent turmoil within, the outer shell triumphs over its opposite and, like a needle with thread, it closes the chasm leaving the darkness behind.

CHAPTER SIX

Who Are We?

What is Normal?

Normality is subjective. My normal is different from yours, yours is different from another and so on. Even my own normal prior to epilepsy changed dramatically by the mental and physical challenges thrown at me. Then, with the addition of FND[2] with seizures, that normal changed yet again and again once more during COVID.

The physical and psychological exploitation I endured in my formative years produced an emotionally stunted woman lacking any confidence in herself. The negative male influences I experienced during that time affected my adult relationships. With no emotional attachments to myself and how I interacted with others, they resulted in poor decisions and toxic relationships throughout my teens and into my forties. But it wasn't until the FND[2] diagnosis that all those past events suppressed for decades and the traumatic experiences in the first four years of my epilepsy, that it hit me how damaged I was inside. It made sense now. Not fostering close friendships for fear of being hurt and preferring to be alone. Hiding in the background, avoiding the spotlight, flying under radars, not wanting my picture taken, uncomfortable with compliments. And yet, I related better with boys than girls. Girls were into make-up and dresses, jewellery, and the latest hairdos. I was not. Boys were the exact opposite, more like me in many ways. They didn't share their feelings. It seemed odd that I could relate better to males considering my negative interactions with them. An overbearing father; the sexual misconduct perpetrated by my friend's father and the newspaper boy. I now believe I sought others like me, the ones who built walls, stayed in the shadows, turned the other cheek, and hid. Kindred spirits of the suppressed. Those who felt unimportant, manipulated, and made fun of. By not acknowledging the feelings of sadness, loneliness, and being unworthy, reduced the pain. Ignoring was better than feeling. Hiding was better than being noticed. I hid my emotions so well; I never developed the ability to know what I was feeling when I was feeling it. I couldn't tell you if I was happy, or even what would make me happy. My emotional thermometer was broken. If I got angry, I'd cry. When I cried, I got angry but didn't know why. I was a mixed up, messed up, disconnected individual who didn't know who she was. It's possible those suppressed emotions from childhood spurred my need to hide my female identity. In my impressionable mind, a girl attracted unwanted attention, her dealings with the male species traumatic. Genetics aside, I wonder if those experiences contributed to my overeating, weight gain, refusal to wear dresses and opting for pants. How I aligned my activities with my brother, played with hot wheels, rode bikes, played war games in the bushes around our house, socializing in groups rather than one-on-one, preferring the safety in numbers. And yet, despite the abusive exposure with the opposite sex, especially those whose job it was to protect and care for me, I felt comfortable hanging with my brother and his friends rather than my female schoolmates. There I was, hovering on the fringe, watching as my brother and his pals worked on their cars. I tagged along to concerts and movies, played cards and board games, always within that safety net of numbers. But at some point, we all moved on, lost touch, and the numbers dwindled. Left to my own devices, I hadn't a clue where to go or what to do and who to do it with. I was a young woman, out of touch with her emotional compass, and unable to make sound relationship decisions. Having grown up suppressing all thoughts and emotions, not knowing how to communicate feelings hadn't prepared me for adulthood.

What you learn during your formative years lays the foundation for how you move through life. Whatever you're exposed to becomes normal, or what you consider to be normal. It doesn't mean it's right or wrong, but what you learned plays a role in who you become, and who you can or cannot trust, and so forth.

We are a speck of sand in an hourglass, our lives a mishmash of events eroded by the passage of time. We are a microdot, a single sliver cut out of a massive orb, mere specks of artwork splattered across the globe. We are microscopic shards of ice floating through life, our particles a living organism of oxygen breathing life. A composite of elements, of oxygen, carbon, and hydrogen, we are invisible, part phosphorus, calcium, and nitrogen. Our bodies made up of potassium, magnesium, sulfur, and chlorine, we are covered by humankind's largest organ, the skin. A brittle core wrapped up in muscle and fat. We are progressive, aggressive and yet in spite of that, our presence is just a brief moment in time.

It wasn't until the FND[2] diagnosis that I was referred to a neuropsychologist. During our sessions we uncovered the root of the

FND[2] with seizures. The childhood trauma, alcohol abuse, toxic relationships, the epilepsy, brain surgeries, commuting to Alberta, the depression, anxiety and inability to release my emotions in a healthy, normal way. And just like a sewer plugged to bursting, the shit hit the fan. A steady stream of fear, anxiety, depression, suicidal ideations, panic, and anger rose to the surface, overwhelming my senses. The massive swirl of crap moving too fast, pushing too hard, was more than my head could handle. The only way it could protect itself was to overload the mainframe, wreaking havoc on the operating system, forcing a complete shutdown.

Spring cleaning; rearranging the old and making it new again.

In therapy we discovered my driving need to shift, clean, move, wipe the screen clean, and start over, was, in fact, my inner psyche looking for new beginnings. A new life. Fresh start. Re-energize my space and therefore myself. It was an urge to transform, shift my surroundings, see life in a new way, clean, crisp, and new. There wasn't anything wrong about it. I'm not crazy or insane. It's a coping mechanism, not a compulsion gone out of control. It's who I am and how I think. Besides, who doesn't want a clean space to live in?

As a child, my mother never worried about me keeping my bedroom clean. My idea of cleaning was to remove every item off the bookshelf, dust and replace the books stacked in alphabetical or numerical order, the largest on the bottom with the smallest on top the spines right-side up so the titles were easy to read. All the baseboards and closet, and bedroom doors wiped down, and windows washed, including the track. Picture frames, every inch of the room wiped and dusted, and, most importantly, reorganized. The bed, dresser, and bookshelf moved, and carpet vacuumed. The configuration changed with every clean. Bed under the window, or moved to the north wall, then the east, but not enough room for the west side. The dresser followed suit, bookshelf in tow. As I got older and moved into my first apartment and all those that followed, my penchant for shifting furniture never left me. I didn't spring clean in the truest sense of the phrase. Mine was a quarterly transaction. And it only got worse.

Dem Walls

Fast forward to my twenties, married and with a kid, I developed a method that eventually backfired thirty years later; a strategy whereby I bypassed, ignored, and buried things that upset me. If I didn't like a situation or person, I cut them out, removing them like a stain on a favourite top. I thought I was strong. Believed it took more courage and strength to walk away than face the problem. My favourite saying became; 'you can only beat your head against a brick wall for so long before you realized it hurt.' The problem was, I barely tapped that wall and then immediately cried uncle. It was far easier to walk around the wall and escape to the other side. And I deployed this theory in every aspect of my life.

It was the series of events from 2006 to 2014, which saw my fortress deteriorate. I left my marriage of nineteen years and became a widow four months later. Boxed up the guilt I felt and stored it away. I hadn't the time or energy to look at it. I had my twelve year old son to look after. Two years later, I would enter into a relationship that cracked the flaky mortar between the bricks of my teetering skyscraper. The drama of combining two families amid teenaged antics, drugs and alcohol, picked away at my wall, destroying it brick by brick. A change in job, and the purchase of a house that was the furthest thing from a home, set the dynamite that blasted a hole through my armour of stone. On Dec 23, 2011, I experienced my first seizure. A full-on funky chicken on the floor of a sweat filled hot yoga studio. The shock of that electrical storm ruptured my essence, altered my state of mind, and changed me. The life I hid sprang forth and hit me square in the face. Emotions flooded and overwhelmed me. Its force knocked me down as it rushed through me and my old mantra 'beating my head against a wall…' came back, and I fled.

[The ongoing stress and theatrics weren't worth the effort. I wasn't happy and the only way to fix it was to sell the house and go.]*
*From *Chapter Two of my memoir, Battles of The Mind.*

THE COVID YEARS—2020—2022

An image so clear yet fades in the distance vanishing from view. Only stark colours remain no hint of lush landscapes once filled with laughter. Imprisoned by glass staring out into a world of fantasy, escaping momentarily only to seek safety once more. Life's essence carries on in private watching nature unfold lifeless yet productive. A virtual existence of day to day holding out for something more.

Sad eyes peering out through sheets of glass silent behind a mask; searching for what it lost.

CHAPTER SEVEN

2020

A Pandemic—Death and Mourning

It's okay to cry and feel disappointed, frustrated, angry, and fed up. It's okay to be sad, to let the emotions flow and feel the muscles relax and release the pent-up tension. Or so I kept telling myself.

With the advent of COVID, we've all experienced trauma to some degree. Whether it's been the fear, dread, or panic of contracting it or the inconsistencies of information about the disease and vaccines. The death of loved ones, family members, and friends. The isolation, anxiety, and depression experienced by thousands, millions globally. Is it no wonder there's been an increase in mental illnesses, including PTSD. I've felt it, experienced the depression and anxiety of COVID combined with my seizure disorders and the genuine fears of contracting it and the potential to increase my seizure activity. I've experienced suicidal ideations as many others have and, fortunately, gotten through it unharmed.

So, is it so far-fetched or hard to believe that we've all been physically and mentally impacted?

COVID arriving so soon after our move and my FND² with seizures diagnosis thwarted any attempts at controlling them. The untimely death of our mother on April 1st ignited the already volatile situation. We were still learning about FND² with seizures and how it related to me and my epilepsy. Already frustrated by the continuation of epileptic events, the addition of another seizure disorder only confused the issue. Which was which? How can we tell the difference? We can't. How do we manage this new tormentor? Tears of frustration were a daily occurrence, as was the anger, anxiety, and loneliness.

Epilepsy alone was isolating enough. Add in a global pandemic, I might as well crawl under a rock. Our move, the beginning of a new life of promise and safety, blown to bits. The guilt of leaving my mother behind now turned to grief, mourning her loss. If I thought 2015 was a write-off, 2020 was a shit storm! Sickness, death, isolation, fear, loneliness, grief, helplessness, all wrapped within a surreal emptiness the likes of The Twilight Zone. It was too much. Just way too much for my damaged brain to handle.

The seizures began. Their momentum increasing to where I was experiencing them every two weeks. In and out of hospitals, ambulances, and doped up on Ativan, Midazolam, and large infusions of Dilantin. We didn't know which seizure struck; the EMTs didn't know, and neither did the ER docs. My defenceless body was overloaded with brain numbing drugs to still the eruptions of mind and body. I became a toxic waste dump for benzos and anti-seizure medications.

Another year has passed and so much has changed. Moving from my birthplace, leaving some family behind, but now closer to others. So now what? Since 2015, my so-called year of new beginnings that wasn't, I placed little faith into a year without hospitals. From March 15, 2015, to September 12, 2019, I spent 177 days under a microscope. Spent 11% of my time in the hospital being poked and prodded. You'd think after three surgeries and two intracranial monitorings, it would have been enough and yet, if I never had another epileptic seizure, the FND^2 would still be there. So, what does the future hold for me? Do I even want to know??

Journal Entry, January 12, 2020

I just want to sleep. I'm so sad, lonely, and depressed. All I want to do is cry. I can't believe I had a seizure in our gym. What was I doing? How long was I there? Was it a functional seizure or an epileptic one? So many unanswered questions. So, I can't go to the gym alone? I was doing so well. I want to scream until my throat hurts.

Journal Entry, January 16, 2020

I met the Ophthalmologist, Dr. Malcolm for the first time today. My Optometrist back in BC had diagnosed early stage glaucoma and prescribed eye drops. To continue monitoring the eye pressure, my new eye doctor referred me to Dr. Malcolm. *Sigh.* Another doctor to add to my growing list. *C'est la vie.*

Journal Entry, April 16, 2020

Mom's death affected me more than I knew it would. Despite the physical distance between us, her leaving only added to the forced isolation of COVID. She'd been my 'go to' friend when needing a sympathetic ear. It's been over two weeks now and it's so difficult not to pick up the phone and call her, share a funny tidbit or picture by text.

Some days feel like they're frozen in time while others sped by without my noticing. She wasn't around to share the good days, my achievements, and failures. I stopped myself from calling her about my news about UPLIFT[7] working with Dr. Samson and Donna, supporting individuals with epilepsy suffering from depression and anxiety. How we were the first in Western Canada to offer the program. She was always the first person to know what was going on in my life. It was surreal to realize I could no longer talk to her, couldn't see her, share anything, laugh or cry over silly things, that I was truly alone. She was my best friend, my only friend who understood me. Now she was gone, and I miss her terribly.

Journal Entry, April 23, 2020

I met Dr. Samson on Zoom today. She went over the process and training required for UPLIFT[7] and felt I'd be a good fit to cofacilitate. My experiences with uncontrolled seizures, depression, and anxiety, and willingness to help others is exactly what she's looking for. Not a combination I'd normally put on a resume.

Project UPLIFT[7] was designed specifically for people with epilepsy who suffer from depression and anxiety. It's a combination of cognitive behaviour therapy and mindfulness techniques. Originally designed to be conducted over the phone, it's now being offered through Zoom. The program consists of eight weekly sessions covering topics related to depression, anxiety, negative thinking, and teaching relaxation techniques to reduce stress and promote awareness of body in connection to feelings.

The next training group starts tomorrow, April 24th. It's eight sessions on Zoom, provided by the University of Washington. So strong was my desire to help others like me, I took every opportunity I could to volunteer and readily agreed to participate. With the lock downs from COVID, running a program such as this online was the perfect solution and fed my desire to help.

What I hadn't known at the time was how helpful UPLIFT[7] would prove to be for my own state of mind. The learning tools to reduce the anxiety over my seizures and the depression which followed every event would be a major influence in controlling my seizures. There was such a need for it with the added isolation and fear of death from an illness no one really knew much about. It helped me to realize my so-called 'realist' attitude was really a form of negative thinking and combined with the inability to identify the difference between thoughts and emotions. I was caught in a vicious cycle of anxiety—negativity—overly emotional—state of depression.

Mom / Nana August 1933—April 2020 RIP

Journal Entry, May 5, 2020—
A conversation…

I miss you, Mom. I know it hasn't been easy dealing with me these past five years, but you knew I loved you. I'm so alone knowing you aren't there that I won't hear your voice or your laughter. Mom, I'm struggling. I don't want to talk about or deal with your estate. I'm wishing away another year, thinking the next will be better. You'd think I'd know by now that isn't the case. Every year seems to be a repeat of the last.

My seizures have changed from the big bangs once or twice a year to multiple eruptions, each one taking another piece of me away. They're altering my moods and outlook on life, sinking me deeper into the mire. The days of positive thinking, looking for brighter days, are now obscured. My life centred around my head and the dysfunctional neurons exploding as they will. Even with Foothills in the distance and close to those that can help me doesn't remove the feelings of helplessness, sadness, disappointment, and despair. The anger, frustration, hate and resentment have weakened my resolve. I can't seem to overcome the anxiety and fear. I'm trapped within my own pity party. The why me? Why do I have to be so different? Why can't I be a normal textbook case?

Journal Entry, May 10, 2020

Happy Mother's Day, Mom. It feels strange that I can't pick up the phone and wish you the best on this special day. You finally got your wish that we do not spend any money on you. But like I always said, a child cannot *not* buy your mother something on Mother's Day. It's an unwritten law of nature.

I tried to bury myself, wanting to avoid thinking about you today. The sense of loss is too raw. The wound hasn't stopped bleeding to allow it to scab over. It still feels like a dream, a foggy nightmare that won't end. Feeling you're still here and I can reach out and touch you haven't faded. It's difficult to acknowledge and accept that we won't talk anymore. Wanting to call or text you is so strong, but you're not there to receive the messages. I always knew your passing would hurt. We could talk about anything, or at least we could, up until five years ago. The strain of my epilepsy and the sense of loss and helplessness affected us both. We drifted apart in our own seas of frustration. Yours as a mother who couldn't help her daughter and me as an adult whose life was destroyed.

I'm sorry for all the pain I inflicted and regret how I behaved. Whether it was the meds or the illness itself, please know my love for you remains within me. Locked away in its own special place, living within my soul, a part of my spirit. I love you, Mom. Always have and always will.

Journal Entry, May 14, 2020

2020 feels just like 2015. The hospital visits and seizures these last five months were like déjà vu. I thought my new tools would help to manage my stress and cope with the anxiety. I guess not. I am trying, and there's not much else I can do to overcome some psychological/emotional baggage my mind can't seem to unpack. I thought once we settled into our new home and the stress of moving dissipated, I could move forward but with COVID and Mom dying suddenly I'm back to waiting. Waiting to see if the therapy will reduce the functional seizures, preferably eliminate them. Not until then will we know if the surgeries made any difference.

Today I'm on the other side of the looking glass, longing for home. The tall spires of metal and glass were across the river waiting for my return. This 'Chateau' that tends to my needs, while familiar, is not where I should be. My life shouldn't be all about doctors, hospitals, needles, and tests. It should be free to wander like leaves swirling in a breeze lazily skimming along. But the burden of the mind weighs heavily on the physical and emotional wellbeing. The ability to rise requires superhuman strength and determination. Traits that are in short supply. My toolbox is almost empty, its contents forgotten each time I have knocked it over, searching for the right implement. A desolate spirit living within, pushing aside the inner soul, determined to survive. Shadows fill the place where a positive glow of energy had been, the brightness now reduced to grey. Silent. Still. Motionless.

I'm pushing people away. Don't feel like talking. Crawling inside my shell, wanting everyone to go away.

Journal Entry, May 25, 2020

Another month is almost over. Half the year just about gone and more visits to hospitals than months so far. I hope this isn't my new norm. I thought moving here would reduce the seizures, not increase them. But then, who knew COVID would be around and Mom would pass on. It's a real shitty year so far. It's like the previous ten years rolled into one enormous pile of crap. Will it ever get better? It seems like I've been on a ride to hell for the last fifteen years. I don't expect life to be easy, but, come on, haven't I had more than my fill of misfortune and grief? From leaving my husband, his death four months later, followed by a toxic relationship, my epilepsy, glaucoma, and, now the functional seizures. Someone really has it in for me, or a previous life has come back to torment me. I'm tiring of it all.

It's difficult to stay motivated, positive, or focused. I just want the world to go away and leave me alone. Let me find some peace and serenity. The life outside interferes with the calm I need to manage my stress and anxiety. These constant disturbances pressing in on me increase the worries and strain of maintaining the status quo. Never thought I'd be living like this. Propelled into a strange world of retirement but unable to reap the rewards. My travel destinations are doctors' offices, clinics for testing, and emergency departments and hospital wards. These shouldn't be a concern at fifty, more like seventy-five or eighty. I'm a burden to my son and regardless of his desire to take care of me, his life has stalled.

Journal Entry, May 27, 2020—Follow up appointment with Dr. Malcolm

I'm a bit nervous to see Dr. Malcolm today. He told me at the last appointment to be prepared for the possibility of laser eye surgery if the pressure hasn't dropped. I had cataract surgery back in 2006 and wasn't concerned. The issue for me, was going blind. As it was, the pressure was still hovering around eighteen and we went ahead with the laser treatment and added a second eye drop.

Journal Entry, May 30, 2020

Why can't this go away? Why am I still broken despite the treatments? I realize I'm not alone, but why do I feel so helpless? Am I depressed? I guess it's possible. I certainly don't enjoy the activities I used to or even perform the everyday tasks as I used to. Cleaning isn't a priority anymore. A few crumbs on the counters, floors that need sweeping, tables, and pictures covered in dust no longer disturb me, my need for perfection, gone. I shifted my priorities. Battling a chronic illness has depleted my energy and shifted my focus inwards. My only priority is to exist. Everything else is secondary.

Journal Entry, June 1, 2020

I feel like an ant climbing a sand hill in a windstorm. Every grain I step on slides away, taking me with it. I'm tired of the battle and the wasted energy. Tired of everything. I'm mentally numb and physically empty, sunk into a hole and don't want to get out. It's just too much work. I've lost the ability to feel pleasure. The last six months have been rough on everyone, but with COVID and Mom gone, and my FND[2] diagnosis, this move to Calgary wasn't what I had envisioned for our new life.

Both Drs. Young and Harper are concerned about my mental state. My depression scores are the highest they've ever been, as are my anxiety levels. I'll be meeting with Dr. Harper weekly for a while. They both agree my poor quality of life and mindset are a perfect recipe for the functional seizures. And Dr. Young will place a referral to the psychiatrist,

Dr. McKay, to review my antidepressant medication which hasn't been monitored for coming up to a year now.

Journal Entry, June 4, 2020

Today, we officially started our first UPLIFT[7] group. It would be the start of many more to come. From June 2020 to February 2021, Dr. Sophie and I worked together providing support throughout the early days of COVID.

Journal Entry, June 8, 2020

I don't believe I've ever been so low in a mood before. I've wrapped myself within my walls. And now I'm faced with the reality of early-stage glaucoma, I'm afraid of going blind. Of all my senses to lose, sight is my biggest fear. Not to see the ocean or river, the mountains, blue sky, would kill me. I derive so much pleasure by watching nature and all that which is my inspiration for poems. I would rather lose my ability to taste or feel, even hear over the inability to see. Perhaps I'm overreacting, but am I? My life has been a shit pile growing larger as each year passes. I've grown weary of the battles and obstacles, the wrong, or bad, decisions, my constant feeling of climbing a hill made of quicksand. Moving towards a destination I can't reach. Standing still, within a state of perpetual motion.

Journal Entry, June 9, 2020

My body is falling apart. I hate this year and everything it represents. Death, isolation, and fear. After years of burying emotions, my subconscious has risen with such force, it's consumed my body. Basic functions of seeing, hearing, and feeling have altered. I'm controlled like a puppet, obeying the wishes of its master. My mind has lost control.

Journal Entry, June 13, 2020

My mood is better but still sits in a hole. It's not as dark as it was, a little lighter maybe, but still heavy. I don't miss friends and haven't had a social life for quite some time. But I miss the interaction with the doctors and nurses who form my inner circle. When you spend so much time in hospitals as I do, it becomes a form of recreation. Like going to camp or on a weekend getaway. Sadly, I'd rather visit Foothills than go to the library.

Journal Entry, June 16, 2020

My mind seems calmer this past week. I'm not overreacting to every brief twinge and I'm getting better at turning off negative thoughts. I resumed my writing and haven't had a seizure in three weeks. If I'm honest with myself, I'm relieved the recent seizures were FND[2] but the guilt and worry are still there. I worry about Devon being forced into a caregiver role and feel guilty about my ER visits adding pressure on an already overloaded system. Which isn't justified. Why do I feel this way? Why do I believe I'm not worthy of the attention or sick enough to warrant care?

Journal Entry, June 22, 2020

I was slow to get up, dozing in a state between consciousness and not. I couldn't wake up. Waves of sensation from stomach to head and back, that combination of queasy nervous energy rising and receding repeatedly. Like g-forces attacking my gut and bursting forth, only to disappear into the next. The scent of nausea was just a hint, more memory than reality. It transported me back to December 2014. That week of a 'flu' that wasn't. I don't know how long it went on. Maybe thirty minutes, an hour, fifteen minutes or five? Was it anxiety? A functional seizure? Hunger pains? Or simply that I had to pee? Regardless, for one who'd slept almost ten hours, I shouldn't be tired.

My depression has worsened and I've had thoughts of 'what if I went over the balcony railing? What would happen?' I didn't want to kill myself; I just wanted to let go. To be free. Free from seizures and COVID to float without worries, not plagued with what ifs. To stop focusing on what my body is or isn't doing. I don't want to look out my window at Foothills in the distance wondering when my next visit will be. I shouldn't think of it as a second home, it's just a hospital where sick people go. I pray for the day Dev can move forward without fearing the next seizure will kill me. It isn't much of a life for a man in his twenties; chained to a parent out of worry and obligation. The move to Calgary was a necessity for me. The resulting baggage Devon must carry an unfortunate result.

Journal Entry, June 26, 2020

Why does everything take effort? Not the effort of moving or thinking, but simple stuff like ordering patio furniture, booking a flight, getting from point A to B without complication. In my depressed state, completing a task takes too much effort. Any roadblocks, hiccups, or bumps along the way overwhelm me, eliminating the motivation required to execute them. I guess that means I've spent my whole adult life in a state of depression. Or maybe it's the extra work needed to breakthrough the barriers I erected.

I consider myself a realist, bordering on a fine line of negativity and cynicism. Life was a bowl of lemons, not cherries. To expect anything sweeter would be an improvement. But to get one's hopes up only to be trampled on causes emotional pain, which my fortress pushes away. As a teenager, I would wander from group to group, choosing when to move on to avoid rejection. I hovered on the outer fringes unattached, a shadow that appeared and disappeared like a cloud blocking out the sun. To some extent, I continued my nomadic life as an adult. Never allowing too many inside my hula-hoop for fear they'd destroy my defences. In my current mindset, my bubble had morphed, transforming into a hardened shell. The person within battered and broken, needing more protection than in the past. The focus moved inwards, leaving others behind, making room to rebuild the walls that eroded.

Journal Entry, July 1, 2020

I have been dormant for the last few days. Had to force myself to get dressed and find reasons to go out. My wavy, anxious feelings have resurfaced. Probably the stress and anxiety of our upcoming trip to the coast. A part of me doesn't want to go. No disrespect to Mom but going makes it real. Final. To bury her ashes and rummage through her possessions means she's never coming back. That she's gone for good. I don't know if I'm angry at her or just sad, depressed, and grieving. I feel empty and lost.

Journal Entry, July 5, 2020

I always feel better after talking with Dr. Harper. Whether it's the therapy or just having someone who understands. Family and friends have a hard time separating the old connection from now, just as I struggle.

In less than two months, it will be a year since we moved. I can't believe the time has passed so quickly. So much has occurred. Trips to the ER and SMU finding our new home, and Mom dying. Reconnecting with my old GP, Dr. Alisen. Meeting Dr. Harper and now assisting Dr. Samson with UPLIFT[7]. Seizure activity increased as 2020 started, the FND[2] being more prevalent than my epilepsy. I guess that's a good thing but doesn't change the fact I'm having seizures. This emotional side of me is harder to control than the physical.

Journal Entry, July 6, 2020

I had a seizure yesterday. Felt wavy, nauseous, some pressure, and was unable to focus. I think it stopped and started a few times. Dev would know. He got part of it on video. Looks like the left side of my mouth was twitching, my lips smacking. Not sure how long it was before the Ativan took effect and the pressure released.

Our patio furniture arrived! Finally, a nest for me to escape to. I can meditate, read, practice mindfulness exercises, and watch the world below. Looking out over the buildings and concrete, it reminds me of South Pointe near White Rock. People moving about their day, oblivious yet so very aware of those around them. A sense of belonging during isolation.

UPLIFT[7] should start up again in October. I can start my volunteering at Foothills soon and spend more time writing.

Journal Entry, July 7, 2020

    I sat on the balcony, cup of coffee in hand, and felt the morning sun on me. A bit on the chilly side, but pleasant enough under my throw. Summer has just begun, there'll be plenty more days to enjoy. Thankfully, UPLIFT[7] runs until July 23rd, and with my appointments with Dr. Harper, I should be okay until the fall. I don't know when I'll hear from Dr. McKay's office, but that will add to my arsenal. It will probably mean more drugs or an alteration to my Escitalopram, but whatever. I'm tired. Tired of working around doctor appointments, arranging activities based on other people's schedules. I don't want to do it anymore. I want to hibernate and come out when I want to, not because someone else desires it.

    I've had fourteen seizures since the new year. An average of one every two weeks. Whether they were functional seizures or my epilepsy, that's a lot. Could be worse, but not my best either. I had seventeen throughout all of 2019. But to be fair, COVID wasn't around. Mom was still with us, and I was in familiar surroundings. The stress of selling and moving caused those. All the years of fear, frustration, anxiety, and depression broke the dam. Am I in some sort of transition? Must I go through a process of decompressing before throwing out the garbage just so I can move forward? I'm tired. I don't want to struggle through this nightmare anymore. Tired of working so hard only to get nowhere, or so it feels. I don't think I really know, or I've forgotten, how to be happy. Is it because I've always felt inferior to others? That I don't add up? Believe I'm not smart enough, pretty enough, not popular enough, incompetent, clumsy, and too loud?

Journal Entry, July 8, 2020

I slept over ten hours. The longest I have in… I don't know how long. My body feels weak, my head is sore, possibly weather related. I don't know. Spent the morning dusting, vacuuming and finished cleaning my bathroom. I'm exhausted, my limbs heavy encumbered by a gravitational force. Nausea, headaches, and achy body had me believing I'd come down with COVID.

My inability to control the FND^2 is taking a toll on Dev. He's having a rough time coping with them and figuring out which type it is. I can't imagine being in his shoes, living with the worry and fear that I could die. It's not how I pictured his life.

Once this business with Mom is done, I'm not going back to the coast. There's no need. I will continue my relationships as I have, by text, phone, e-mail, and messenger. I'm staying put. My desire to travel is dead. It holds no pleasure for me. It is a chore to arrange flights, pet boarding, hotels, and costs money I no longer wish to spend.

ature*Journal Entry, July 9, 2020*text

I'm back to over-examining every twinge, movement, or wave inside my head. Thinking about the future must stop as does dwelling on the past. I've come a long way these last five years, not the route I would have chosen, and not the happy ending we all thought, but I have made progress. I no longer lose awareness with every seizure and my regiment of pills has dropped drastically. Nine per day compared to the twenty-one

I had been pushing down my throat. Yes, I have FND[2] with seizures but therapy, not drugs, is the treatment and there's a higher rate of success.

Journal Entry, July 11, 2020

Another week and Dev's twenty-six, wow. I'm stunned at the passing time and all the events that have occurred since his birth. Moving to his dad's childhood home. Leaving my marriage after nineteen years. In charge of myself for the first time and only my son to care for. The disastrous relationship with Daniel. My second liberation only to end a year later. My doctors replaced friends, and hospitals, labs, and clinics, my social life. My son, from child to caretaker.

Most of the recent seizure activity stems from emotions, not a physical eruption from the release of pressure. They're real, not make believe and no less debilitating than my epilepsy. And I must quit thinking I caused them and feeling guilty when they occur. As with my epilepsy, I am doing all I can to control them. Meditating and acknowledging my feelings. The sadness, anger, a depressed state of mind, the guilt, fear, worry, grieving the loss of self and my mother. I'm tired and bored. I don't know what to do. Where to find pleasure, how to achieve happiness. I just don't know.

Journal Entry, July 12, 2020

Dev and I went for a long walk yesterday. Five miles. We went to the Safeway in Kensington. We only needed a few things, and it's ten times further than the one at the corner. No hills, a peaceful walk. I'm glad we didn't rent over there. I like our little slice of the city. The sun on the balcony each morning returning early afternoon to say good evening. Sitting out there this morning with the sun warming my face, eyes closed listening to music with a breeze passing by, I could imagine I was on the pier back in White Rock. Standing at the end of that grand walkway staring out at sparkling waves rippling across a sheet of blue-green glass. The beaches. White Rock and Crescent are the only places I ever felt at peace. Where I emptied my soul, shared my secrets and pain. I miss them, but I'm slowly finding solace from the view of my balcony. A mixture of concrete and metal dotted with green trees and rolling hills in the background.

Journal Entry, July 13, 2020

I'm enjoying the peaceful mornings out on my balcony. A cup of coffee in hand, Kobo, or journal, headphones, iPod, meditating, or whatever I'm in the mood for. Just relaxing, watching, and listening to the surrounding activity is soothing, more so than just meditating. The classical violins and cellos are calming, like swinging, gently swaying back and forth, lost in the moment. Floating on the air, like a ballerina moving in my head, graceful, light, beautiful. Mesmerizing. I should track all the days I listen to classical music to see if it has any effect on my seizure activity. Some research states listening to certain Mozart compositions can reduce seizure activity, but I haven't read whether it's only piano or some other instrument. I'm no connoisseur of this medium but would

suspect the soothing lilting sounds could make a difference.

Journal Entry, July 15, 2020

Having my patio chairs now has made a difference in my moods. Listening to violin and cello music, drinking coffee, and watching life unfold below is soothing. I've taken to sitting out there in the evening as life winds down. I find it more relaxing than the meditations.

Reality checks are becoming a daily thing. My tendency to jump to the worst conclusions has been detrimental to my mental well-being. I must stop it! They are not facts. They only take me away from today and transport me to a place and time that does not exist. To let them run rampant wreaks havoc on a mind already fragile.

Journal Entry, July 21, 2020

I'm feeling better, or at least that's what I'm telling myself. My left arm and hand are not vibrating like they were. It's still there, the numbness remains but not as strong only noticeable when I touch my face or my right hand. Otherwise, it's as if they don't exist the outer layer removed, leaving the bones picked clean of flesh, muscle, and nerves. The nervous energy within has dissipated like water dried up by the blistering sun and replaced with a stillness of the aftermath of a raging wildness bent on destruction. The eye of the storm is peaceful yet unnerving, the constant threat to the outer layer pierces the serenity of the moment. To stay in the present takes work. Looking backwards at past events which cannot hurt me is a hard habit to break. My life has evolved to where I'm imprisoned behind a series of chambers, and to unlock the gates and set them free scares me.

Journal Entry, July 23, 2020

Today is the last UPLIFT[7] session for this group. I'm learning new tools to help manage my anxiety and despondent mindset. But I'm not naïve to think they'll cure these issues, just like my seizures won't ever disappear. The functional seizures are manageable and could go away, but I doubt that I'll ever be seizure free. Not until they develop a new procedure, medication, or device, will I achieve any peace of mind. I can hope the seizures don't worsen and the three surgeries achieved some success. However, I must deal with the emotional aspects of this illness and not so much the physical, which in a lot of ways, is far more challenging. Physical recovery is measurable whereas, the emotional state is in constant flux. It is not stagnant, is always changing as we move through life. Every second of each day it evolves, shifts, and morphs into new feelings.

Journal Entry, July 24, 2020

In another month, we will have been a year in Calgary. It hasn't been a smooth ride, that's for sure. Bounced and jerked around on an angry Bronco or Raging Bull would be an apt description. I don't regret moving. I'm happy that I'm where I should be; close to my doctors and a medical system that can care for me. While my seizures have not reduced, I have access to the emotional support necessary to help manage them. Because of the emotional stress of the last two years, we cannot determine if my surgeries have made an impact. Maybe in time we will know, but until then, I will continue my therapy and regular checkups with Dr. Young and take part in research studies and volunteer. UPLIFT[7] has given me a great platform to support others like me while gaining the knowledge and tools to help in my own search for peace.

Where I had the ocean before I now have the rolling hills of Nose Hill Park to preoccupy my mind while listening to traffic and wildlife focusing on pitch and tone not vehicle type or species of mammal.

Journal Entry, July 28, 2020

I love listening to classical cello. The sound is rich. How the bow moves across the strings, like skates on ice, calms me. The music cradles me like a newborn gently rocked to sleep. Visualizing the movements of bow and fingertips on strings and rich tones shifts my thoughts away from seizures. Only three seizures since May. A slight improvement from the every other week it had been.

Journal Entry, July 30, 2020

It's warm now. Thank God for the central air! I've felt a great weight on me. Could be the pain and headaches that have tormented me these last few days. The changing pressure, I guess. Or it's the sadness creeping in as we get closer to September.

I'm back into my cycle of despair, brief enjoyment, sadness, and then back into despair. My new tattoo is the one thing, the only thing, that I look forward to right now. A tribute to mom. The White Rose of York surrounded by Mom, Nana, 1933 to 2020. My way of honouring her memory.

I'm stuck in a bubble, floating, nowhere, struggling to burst free, only to be trapped in the next. I'm surrounded by tiny molecules bubbling around me. Each in their own fight to reach the surface and consume me.

The cello music, sitting on my balcony staring at the shifting landscape, the sounds of man and nature colliding, is therapeutic. The steady hum of tires over pavement combined with the beat of machinery as workers toil in the heat is rhythmic. Distinct tones and decibels are like sounds of waves crashing onto the shore, while planes soar above. Magpies, geese, and robins calling from their perches. Stories above the hustle of people, where winds move freely, carrying the noises away.

The weird dreams are back. The ones that include people and places from the past. From twenty years ago and more. I don't remember them except for the feelings of disappointment, disgust, and anger, and I don't know what else. People I've left behind who had upset or disappointed me or let me down. Those I admired, cared for, and hated. A mixture of unusual ingredients without a specific recipe. Like Vaseline on glass, smearing the view, blurring it beyond the familiar.

Journal Entry, August 3, 2020

Had a severe seizure last night while watching a hockey game. I thought it was the game itself, but now that I think about it, it was emotionally triggered. Yesterday was four years since my first surgery. Today is five years since the seizure on my sister's boat put me in the Sullivan District Hospital for three weeks. This one was different from the others. The pain in my head was excruciating. I don't know how long it lasted or if Dev got it on video. I think I dribbled or frothed, and he gave me one Ativan. It started, stopped, and started up again, I think. Slept nine hours or so and felt like a used punching bag that's lost its stuffing. My neck is stiffer than it had been, but tolerable. I think I will skip watching hockey for now to see if that makes any difference. The movement, double vision, and Sportsnet's 3D logo flashing across the screen disturbs my eyes.

I guess my emotional state and potential for seizures will rise as we approach our trip to the coast and the interment of Mom's ashes. I must control this thing buried within me. To release the smoke before the flames, take hold. To curb my tendencies to hoard my feelings and tuck them away in boxes and bins sealed up for permanent storage. Calm the energy which wants to escape. It's taken years to build these walls to keep the negativity and pain away. Stones placed strategically to strengthen the fortress against invaders. The mortar that binds them made of cement and steel has somehow cracked. The physical weight of my tower of isolation has become too great. It is inevitable that it shall fall, one piece at a time.

Journal Entry, August 8, 2020

We've been pretty good about going for walks every other day. Sometimes it's three days in between our outings, but at least we're moving. I've been using the band weights to work on my core. I should do it twice a week at a minimum but struggle to drum up the motivation. Once a week is better than nothing, I guess, and anytime spent is time taken away from idleness and overeating.

Journal Entry, August 10, 2020

Wavy feelings are happening lately, not the anxious ones, but actual waves, like floodgates opening an inch, then closing as the water rushes to pour out. It's probably nothing. Just the anxiety as we approach September and the upcoming trip to the coast. That, and my double vision hasn't improved. I'm of the opinion that when the eye pressure reduces, it's making it worse. Unfortunately, I won't know the cause until October. Oh, my, it's chilly out here this morning.

Journal Entry, August 11, 2020

I've been feeling pretty good. Distracting myself with music and organizing our collection of coins. Reading, writing, eating healthier, and trying to exercise more. My meditations have changed to include the soothing tones of the cello. I try to sit on the balcony once a day, if not more, listening to the hum of traffic and cello, the movements of life down below. There's been moments of sadness where tears have fallen, and the energy flows from my body. Anger or annoyance has created tension in my jaw, neck, and shoulders, the muscles intent on turning to stone. I try to focus on my breathing. The steady, rhythmic breaths allowing the blood to flow throughout my body without hindrance. To reign in those negative thoughts and stop them from casting lies and creating stories that aren't true. Thoughts can produce wonderful things. But when they attempt to take over and control the future, they become destructive. I must remind myself my thoughts are not facts. They do not exist, couldn't breathe on their own if released. They're merely wishes, dreams and nightmares from a land of make believe, and myth. Neither liquid, solid, or gas, they're just spirits within a mind that roam free, unbidden, and not welcome.

Journal Entry, August 14, 2020

If it had only been the seizure and maybe seeing or hearing a few things, I wouldn't have questioned it. But the smells? Those haven't been present in years. There may have been a hint of an odour starting, but nothing notable enough to jot down. Better safe than sorry, I guess.

Are these from the epilepsy or are the functional seizures mimicking these sensations to mock me? They've all been brief, separate occurrences, not linked to one or the other. It's the stress. Stress of COVID, my eyes, going to the coast, my hands, and the seizures.

I must allow myself to feel sad and to grieve. Not only the loss of mom, but everything else. Losing freedom, going to the movies, attending concerts and sporting events, no swimming, soaking in a hot bath, not driving or working. The complete loss of control and independence. Emotions just below the surface lurking under the flesh, swimming through veins, touching every organ. To dam them up and restrict the flow is impossible. They will seek the weakest part and push against its wall until it bursts wide open.

Journal Entry, August 15, 2020

The year is slipping by. If it weren't for my seizure logs and journals, and appointments, there'd be nothing to prove they existed. Another ten days and it's been a year since we moved here. Twelve months. Wow! Twelve months and I've been in hospital, for all but a few. If I were to count them out, probably the same as last year. This must stop. The 911 calls the trips to emergency. Tests.

2020 has not been a year of hope for anyone. It's been about fear, sickness, and death. Everything's different. Roads are empty, wildlife has emerged and taken over the downtown core. Even the weather is not as it should be. A constant shift in the pattern, fluctuating from warm to cold and stormy. Not the typical fare for this time of year.

I recall walking to the pharmacy when the reality set in. A bustling avenue full of shops, restaurants, and cafes, deserted. The odd car or two and a pedestrian here and there wandering the streets as if asleep. The silence was loud, echoing off buildings; unabsorbed by objects normally there to halt its progress. A village of emptiness with a sense of doom hanging over it. It was surreal. I will never forget how it felt and the vision will stay with me forever. It will be interesting to see how the coast is. If there's the same sense of containment.

Journal Entry, August 16, 2020

Another seizure yesterday. It started with twinkling laser type lights in the left eye and a rapid side-to-side motion so fast; it was a blur. I sat down on the toilet and called out to Dev. I don't know if I stood, then fell forward or remained seated. Dev's e-mail will tell me more. Shaking, maybe? Breathing was difficult, lots of saliva. I recall little else other than throwing up. Woke in emergency and I think my first words were 'where am I'? Other than going to pee and asking for water and a brief conversation with the doctor, I remember little else. They brought me clothes to wear home and let me go. I believe I arrived home around 7 pm. Dev said it started around 10 am. The medics, being loaded on to a stretcher, and leaving the apartment I have no memories of. Arriving at Foothills, transferred to a bed and blood work, a blank. Forty-five minutes, I think Dev said. He couldn't administer any Ativan. The right side of my head had been hitting the floor. My cheek bone and above the eye are tender and looks like bruising starting on the cheek and some scrapes on both big toes and left elbow. From shaking, I guess. Think this was an epileptic, and not a functional seizure, and a doozy. Dozed on and off on the couch until dragging myself to bed. It was around 9 pm and I slept until 7 am? I'm weak, tired, a little out of it.

Journal Entry, August 17, 2020

To say this seizure knocked the stuffing out of me would be like a scarecrow devoid of straw left flapping against a pole in a cornfield. I never got out of my PJs, lazed about reading and listening to music. I wrote a bit about how it felt and what I could remember. It didn't flow like my other pieces. Too recent, I suspect. My thought processes too clinical right now, more fact based. At least I have a framework written. As always after each event, my anxiety escalates, a fear rising from my gut that another will follow. Which is ridiculous, really. Never, in the past, has a second seizure followed soon after a major one. Even before my surgeries, with the worst ones, I went months and years between them, if you include December 2011. So why would it be different now? Yes, I have functional seizures which can erupt at anytime, but I think I have a better handle on that now. I'm not having a seizure every two weeks anymore. Well. This month maybe not. I had one August second, and now on the fifteenth. Oh well. Let's get the next month over with. I'm so done with 2020, done with the functional seizures and epilepsy. I want it all to go away and leave me in peace.

I can feel the burn inside me, the tension and muscles tightening, readying for fight or flight. Tears nestled behind eyes, screaming in pain. It feels hopeless. That I'll never be free of the demon living within my head. It has taken hold of the neurons and cut them as if crafting paper dolls, splicing wires leaving them exposed to a danger waiting to happen.

Why, of the three of us, did it have to be me? Why was I the chosen one and not my siblings? Oh, woe is me. Whatever. Deal with it.

Journal Entry, August 20, 2020

I'm fifty-five today, a senior in some sectors, a spring chicken with silvery grey hair. There won't be a birthday card from Mom this year, or the next, and the next and so on. Won't be one at Christmas either. She was always diligent about getting cards out to those she loved and cared about. It was almost as important as breathing to her.

We are getting closer to our trip to the coast, one more month. I hope that once she's laid to rest and the storage locker emptied, that it will bring the closure we all need. I'm praying it will give me the shift I need to turn the corner and leave my FND^2 behind. As Dr. Harper said yesterday, I may not achieve 100% freedom from them, but if they, like my epilepsy, were even a couple times a year, or less, I could cope with it, maybe. I'm so tired of it all. The episodes, the fear, and anxiety, guilt, although I shouldn't feel it, the depression, and thoughts of death.

I stood there preparing my lunch, knife in hand, hypnotized by the shiny metal of the blade. I wondered what it would be like to jab it into my belly or drag it across my wrists and watch the blood pool and drip. Just like the thoughts of leaping over the balcony railing and letting my body fly, it passed. As these thoughts appear, I think of Dev and how badly it would affect him. I couldn't do it to him. It wouldn't be fair. Must remain strong, if not for myself, for Devon. I must find activities to keep me occupied, distract my thoughts to keep from worrying about seizures. Mustn't let epilepsy or FND^2 rule my life. They are conditions I have, but they're not me. I am laughter, generosity, poetic, creative, organized, and fun. So much more than the misfiring neurons and pent-up feelings locked away in my head. I can no longer be a coward hiding behind her wall of stone and cement. While it's been easier and safer, or so I thought, it hasn't been healthy. This buildup of emotions has created a lake full of eddies swirling about like tornadoes, rendering destruction as it touches the shore. If but for a few cracks in that wall slowly releasing trickles of emotion, the backlog would have laid waste to all that lived behind it. It is time to take it down, stone by stone, chipping away at the cement that binds them and let the river flow freely.

Journal Entry, August 22, 2020

Yesterday, Devon and I walked over to Prince's Island Park and then wend our way through the city streets and grabbed the C-train back. Even with taking the train, I logged over ten thousand steps. It's no wonder I slept as well as I did. Didn't get up until 8am! I had a brief episode before we left. Was in my room when my left hand became tingly and felt as though it would start twitching, and that rising anxious wavy sensation began. I focused on breathing and how my body felt on the chair, feet on the floor, and it subsided. Wonder if it was a borderline panic or anxiety attack? Maybe that's how functional seizures start. The anxiety increases and overwhelms me. The good news today is I've been able to watch a hockey game or two without incident. That's a relief.

Journal Entry, September 4, 2020

I'm feeling better. The anxious wavy lightheaded sensations have mostly stopped. At least they're not occurring daily or multiple times per week. Whether it is the cello and Mozart music or using the skills I've learned from UPLIFT[7], whatever I'm doing seems to work. Now the key is to get through the remaining weeks of September. We leave for the coast in two weeks. That's going to be intense. Seeing the remains of Mom put to ground. Sorting through the storage locker. Hope I can keep it together. I'm sure I can. I have new tools to help me. It'll be fine. Have faith.

Journal Entry, September 12, 2020

I'm stressed over our trip. Whether the flight gets cancelled, having seizures, not wanting to go. My left hand and corner of mouth and even my foot has been tingling. The sensation in my fingers has depleted and I'm dropping things. I hadn't any waves to speak of or floaty, woozy sensations per se. Just the stroke like sensations on my left side. I've been listening to Mozart and cello music almost constantly and I firmly believe they're what's keeping the lid closed. Other than today, I've been sleeping well. I've been awake since 4am; I think. Fell back to sleep for a bit and got up around 7 am. Even yesterday during my Zoom meeting, I felt the increased vibration in my arm. Obviously, I couldn't listen to music but instead focused on grounding myself. Pressing my toes into the floor, bringing attention to my butt on the chair, and twiddling my fingers and rubbing my hands, got me through. It's hard to ignore those sensations, to turn your focus elsewhere while following the surrounding conversations.

Journal Entry, September 18, 2020

We leave tomorrow. I really don't want to go. I don't want to go through the storage locker and bury her. It'll make it real. Final. But I guess that's what I need to get closure. It was different with dad. I wasn't as close. Closer to him in the end than in my childhood, but Mom was my best friend. She didn't like confrontation. She dealt with things in her passive aggressive ways. We were a lot alike. Organized to obsession, comfortable with ourselves and being alone. Similar hobbies. Reading, tv, walks, I used to knit, crosswords and jig saws. Maybe 2020 is my transition year. To tidy up loose ends and cut ties or the umbilical cord to my birth home. All my friendships, what's left of them, have been virtual. Text, phone, messenger. No matter. I have the Alexandra Writing Centre Society and UPLIFT[7] to keep me out of trouble. And my writing, reading, and Dev. My wonderful, awesome, amazing son.

Journal Entry, September 20, 2020

It's Sunday. Arrived yesterday. Tired. Everything looks new yet familiar. Except the beach. The tension in my body seeped away, slowly draining as we got closer to the pier. I felt its arms encircling me, easing the fear and the pain. I felt safe and secure just as I always did. Embraced in her arms, feeling the love and tenderness. It felt like coming home after years lost wandering alone. We walked along the promenade below the hump, the brush and trees grown back after the desecration. The slaughtering of tender vines, soft leaves, bark, branches and thorny bushes. Now lush and alive again, vibrant. My beloved Pier, no longer broken pilons that held cracked boards and splintered timber, now fully restored. Stronger and healthy once again, her beauty held in awe of all those who walk along her feeling the breeze off the water and hearing the gulls cry. Hello, my friend, it's so good to see you up and about. I've missed you but am so happy you're back to your old self. I'm sorry we don't have much time to spend together, next time for sure. Take care and stay safe.

Journal Entry, September 22, 2020

Here I sit at 5:30am hiding out in the bathroom so not to waken Dev. Kind of rings a bell, eh Mom? Four years ago, in a hotel room in Calgary? My first surgery and you were in the bathroom playing Candy Crush. You were afraid the light from the cell phone would wake us. Silly! I'm hiding out to write and keep my mind off coffee. The damn machine is noisy. I'll give it a bit longer and waking Dev or not, I need my caffeine!

I bought a plot near yours yesterday. Under the shade of a tall tree and with a view of the mountains. Three generations close to each other, you, Vanessa, and me with Jim and Carol close by.

You're being put to bed today, Mom. Jim made your urn and it's positively beautiful. A work of art and superior craftmanship. You'd be proud. I have some poems and a story I'll put in to give you some reading material. I think you'll like them. We cleaned out the storage locker yesterday. It was weird to go through your stuff. It felt like I was dumpster diving. Rummaging through discarded belongings tossed away, no longer wanted or needed.

Journal Entry, September 29, 2020

I didn't make it to the funeral, Mom, as I'm sure you noticed. Maybe waking too early. The stress and emotions overwhelmed me. I had a seizure just as we were going to visit your friend Myra. I don't know if it was a functional seizure or the epilepsy. The emergency doctor believes it was an epileptic seizure, but I'm not 100% convinced. The discharge summary says I went into status epilepticus, and they loaded me up with Ativan, Midazolam, and some Propofol? (A sedative, I believe). But if it were a functional seizure, none of those would have halted it, except maybe the Propofol. It could have just run its course. Anyhow, I ended up in the ICU again. Tube down throat and an IV jabbed into my jugular and one in my arm.

I remember being outside the CIBC bank when a sudden need to sit washed over me. Dev said I sat down abruptly on the bench. Then my left arm and leg started twitching. I recall Dev having to straighten me up periodically. I kept leaning to the right, almost falling off the bench. He said I was really fighting it; I think I was trying to ground myself. He asked if I wanted an Ativan. Supposedly I said yes. I don't recall receiving it. I woke in the ICU. Dev read my poems and made sure they and my Mary Martha story went in with your ashes. I felt I should go to the plot to get closure but resisted. If it was a functional seizure, going back to the site where you're buried could set off another one and I just wanted to get home. I saw where you were being placed the day before. That's enough. You're at rest. The locker is empty. Your condo sold. The closure will come from writing my poetry and with the few possessions I've taken to remind me of you. And when it's my time, I'll be just a few feet away—lots of time to catch up then.

This trip will be my last to the coast. The stress of travelling, regardless of the emotional torrents running through me, was too much. I am done with planes and airports, taxis, and hotels. I'm becoming you, mom. No desire to travel, to leave the comforts of home. I crave the routine and familiar surroundings. I'm earthbound now until the Lord takes me.

Journal Entry, October 13, 2020

I'm falling into a funk. Constantly thinking about seizures, watching for signs, worrying over the slightest tingle in my hand or face. I need to chill out and focus on the outside of my body and mind and improve my sleep. It doesn't help I'm waking multiple times during the night.

I've been remiss with my tracking and noting sensations like seeing things. And I haven't been journaling. I need something to relax me and give my subconscious something to focus on. Keeping my mind occupied and controlling my thoughts will keep me from dwelling on the negative and reduce my anxiety. I feel frustration, annoyance, anger mixed in with sadness, guilt, and the grief of mom's passing. Will life just get past this COVID shit and move on? Haven't enough people suffered and died? How much more can we take? Can I make it through? Could we please just get on with living?

Journal Entry, October 23, 2020

It's been a month since my last seizure. The longest I've gone without this year, I believe. No seizures after we moved into our apartment in October 2019 until January 2020. Then every month since COVID and Mom's passing. All the stress and emotional turmoil triggered both the FND[2] and epilepsy. Thank God we're here in Calgary. It's been five-and-a-half years of hell. The added diagnosis of FND[2] with seizures and unable to differentiate between those and epilepsy is frustrating and scary. My quality of life is nonexistent, as is Devon's. The strain on him is exponential. No friends here, unemployed, not going to school, babysitting his mother. It's hard on him.

Journal Entry, December 19, 2020

And as I always did, I ignored the warning signs. I tried to adjust to my new surroundings, but inside I kept moving backwards. The forward momentum I desperately craved was another world away. Blocked off, impenetrable, and unattainable.

Journal Entry, December 20, 2020

I'm convinced I cause my seizures. That I've done something wrong and couldn't do anything to stop them. It was my fault they were there. I was to blame.

Tamping down the piles of trash composed of incompatible materials that wouldn't mix no matter how hard I tried. At some point, it became brittle and broke away. The slippery parts shifted, the movement eventually turning into a greasy ooze. Then, as each layer fell away, the pile that appeared rock solid turned into a river of pain and fear, suffusing everything in a blanket of despair. If I only had the courage to take out each thought, examine them and let myself experience every emotion, it's possible I could've avoided the functional seizures. Maybe.

All those years believing I was a failure. Considered myself ugly, fat, stupid, a screw up, unwanted and incapable of being loved. The negative views I held about myself were astounding. For as long as I can remember, I'd taken the muddy manure of the past and placed it in a sealed container and hid it away. After the seizures started, it never occurred to me to check on it. To make sure the plastic hadn't deteriorated over the years. And it had. Somewhere, a hole had appeared, just small enough for the fears, anxieties, guilt, anger, and depression to wiggle out. For four years, all those emotions contained seeped through that tiny hole. As the force grew, a crack formed. As it gave way, I couldn't hold it back and everything, all of it, filled my senses, overwhelming me. As I tried to fight it, the seizures intensified, became unstoppable. My doctors placed me in therapy, a combination of CBT, grounding techniques, and lots of talking. I searched for books and any information I could find on functional neurological disorders with seizures and, slowly, my thought processes altered, and I learned about emotions like sadness.

CHAPTER EIGHT

2021 And The Shit Keeps Coming

Walls that keep us apart isolated and afraid of an enemy spreading rapidly around the globe. Together we must stand, and fight conquer or die, we hide not by choice. Gone is the laughter of carefree spirits social gatherings a thing of the past. Children without play dates, no school and no tests. Brave souls carry on providing the essentials of life. Oh, to emerge from behind these walls of protection and feel the sun's warmth once again.

Journal Entry, January 7, 2021

I can't believe it's been a year now. COVID has destroyed so many lives, families in mourning earlier than they should, loved ones lost who had more years left in them. I'm glad Mom isn't having to go through this. The only benefit to her passing. I miss her terribly. I'm reminded of her each time I drink my morning coffee or tea. It's her mugs I use now. I made cookies yesterday. I used her old Pyrex bowl and her hand mixer. I've thought of her often this past week. The new year's eves we spent together, bored trying to find something on tv to watch. The World Juniors just finished. I could see and hear her while she watched the games. She really enjoyed them. 'Not the fighting and carryon, like in the NHL. Just clean hockey,' she always said.

I bought a display cabinet from IKEA and all her Royal crown Derby and Hummels have a new home. Her desk sits in my bedroom, with one of her living room lamps on it. It feels good to have 'her' around me. Her essence sits just about everywhere. From kitchen utensils to the china, Hummels, photo, and memory albums, clothes, desk, computer, bits, and bobs, I can feel her here.

My best friend is gone and I've no one to talk to, confide in, laugh, and cry with. My life is here now. Calgary is my home. I won't go back to British Columbia. I'm done with flying.

Journal Entry, January 15, 2021

Another week and it'll be four months since my last seizure. A record. I can't recall the last time I've gone that long. This last year of therapy and cofacilitating UPLIFT[7] listening to Mozart and cello and grounding techniques all positive reinforcements to reach this milestone.

I went through the UPLIFT[7] material and created a calendar entry on Thursdays, as if running an actual session. It will keep my head in the game and remind me to use those tools I need to keep from going over the edge. I haven't been sleeping too well lately. I fall asleep, wake once or twice to pee, then wake up early, like 4 or 5 am. Most days I grab my phone and play games, the odd time my Kobo. I may head towards a crash landing, but not if I can avoid it. It could be I haven't enough to occupy my mind. I should gather my tax slips and send what I have to the accountant. Might as well. No point waiting till the last minute.

Journal Entry, January 17, 2021

My body is empty, as though it purged itself of an alien being. Arms and legs tensed for action, are now weak, hanging limp, and my chest and stomach hollow chambers where food and air pass through. My head is light unburdened by what ifs, now free to float. I'm a human carcass, a shell glued together with ligaments, muscles, and tied up with strings of vessels. My brain, the heart, and soul, orchestrating each thought and movement.

I had a seizure yesterday, my first since September 22, 2020, six days shy of four months. Unfortunate, yes, but promising too. It's the longest I've gone since I was in the SMU back in September 2019. Maybe even as long ago as 2018. I'd have to look back and see. Mind you, I did have periods of wavy head rushes on and off since Christmas. And in October, experienced spells of hearing, smelling, and seeing things. I forgot words and had out-of-body type experiences such as speaking but as if from somewhere else, a type of fishbowl effect. Two days prior, waves hit back-to-back with head pains, a tingly hand and not sleeping well. All clues of the bigger bang to come. I was aware of the seizure but couldn't communicate. The left side drained of energy, overcome with pins and needles. Even my lips lost some sensation, and my eyes were blinking, not rapidly, but faster than usual. A cold sweat of fear, that 'oh shit' rising, swept over me, sometimes overtaken by a g-force sensation within my head. I tried grounding myself, tried listening to the game on tv, focus on my ass on the seat cushion, the air conditioning on my legs. But nothing helped. The rip tide had taken hold, dragging me along. Dev was in the shower when it started, couldn't have heard me even if I yelled. When he saw me, he thought I was asleep. That I was having a seizure hadn't crossed his mind. But when neither hand could grasp his, my eyes remained closed, and no noise escaped my mouth, he became suspicious. Up until then, I hadn't moved, not a quiver, twinge, or twitch. And then the shaking started. Everywhere. Both sides. I tried to still my body to quiet the trembles, but nothing happened. I don't know how long the shaking went on, but my leg and arm muscles were screaming. I felt every contraction in my body as it contorted in pain. Breathing was difficult as fatigue set in. After what seemed like thirty minutes or more, they stopped. My eyes opened. I could see Dev. The Ativan he gave me had worked for a moment. Then it circled back. After a second Ativan it settled down but hadn't left completely. I could still feel it sitting, ready to pounce. With Dev's help, we stumbled down the hall, into my room, and he helped me into bed, gently drawing up the blanket over me. I soon fell into a deep sleep. I slept through the night, rising only once to pee. The strain of jerking muscles was painful, slowing my progress from bed to toilet and back. Not surprisingly, I awoke early. I fell asleep before 9 pm and slept drug induced until 4 or 5 am. Awakening groggy and sore.

Journal Entry, January 19, 2021

Why am I experiencing these panicky wavy feelings? Why now, after I mastered the techniques of relaxing and relieving my stress? Christmas is over. No pressing matters. All my ducks are in a row, or so I thought. COVID doesn't help, but after a year, we should be used to it, shouldn't we? The social distancing, mask wearing, zoom and phone appointments and lock downs are part of everyday life. Our 'new normal'. I'm reading and working on core exercises at least once per week. Resumed my listening to Mozart. I got away from it for a while when I discovered the classical cello. Dev and I are walking two to three times a week and I restarted FitnessPal.

I'm so disappointed about the seizure the other day. Was it a functional seizure? I Don't know. I gave up trying to tell the difference. Does it really matter when one is as bad as the other? Do I need the Ativan? I don't know, but it stopped and circled back. It's so frustrating. I'm angry and envious of those who had surgery and are free of their tormentor while I'm subjected to both. Why have I been so blessed? Do I feel sorry for myself? Damn rights I do! I'm sad, angry, frustrated, fed up with it all, anxious, and depressed. Part of me still believes I created this, that I crave attention, want people to feel sorry for me. But I don't really believe that. I'm just tired of the 'I cannot.' I can't do this or that's too much for me to handle. That and other than my hand there's no outward signs, it's all just in my head a lie, made up and make-believe. Fantasy, not reality and if it weren't for COVID, would I be seizure free? Obviously, mom's passing would have caused some seizures, but aside from that, could 2020 have been a stellar year? Only one or two seizures instead of what, twenty or more? Maybe I should try to interact more with others? Maybe weekly meet ups with like-minded individuals are what I need. Devon is doing that with his Discord buddies and playing games online. I can see an improvement in his mood, and his weekly check in for diet and nutrition is helping too. It's nice to see him interact with others besides me. I hope when his course starts in April or May, that it's in-person versus online. Being in-person will give him the opportunity to meet new people and make some friends. Maybe by the fall I'll be volunteering at Foothills. If I had that and UPLIFT[7], I could help others and won't have time to think about the seizures. Maybe I should focus on other things, like organizing and laminating my recipes, sorting through my file folders, gather tax stuff to send to the accountant. The more mundane tasks of everyday life. And possibly stop reading so many seizure books and spend more time on fiction.

Journal Entry, January 21, 2021

My body feels trashed. Lower back is almost as painful as my worse kidney infection back in my twenties. Sore legs, headaches, and tired. I slept over eight hours; I think. The last two days I've slept longer than the three nights before the seizure. Is that what it takes to get a decent night's sleep? Seize, get drugged up and reap the benefits of a better sleep for days after? No thanks. I'd rather bypass the assault on my body, the trip to emergency and the drugs. Maybe I should try drinking chamomile tea before bed, that could help relax me. That and my hot showers.

Yesterday, I thought of swallowing a handful of my meds to see if that would end it all. To stop this crazy cycle of seize-drugs-anxiety-depression-worry-fear. If this last one wasn't an epileptic event, then maybe a combination of both? I don't believe it was just a functional seizure.

Journal Entry, January 22, 2021

My hand won't stop tingling. It surges, ebbs, and surges. It's annoying and, of course, concerns me. The constant thoughts of 'is a seizure starting'? only exacerbates the anxiety sitting below the surface, just waiting to breach. Maybe part of it is I'm not working on my book or writing poetry. I thought taking a break from memoir writing would help reduce my constant worries about seizures. Sticking my head in the sand

and avoiding the subject obviously isn't working. Maybe rewriting my poems could be helpful.

Distraction. I need distractions. Sorting recipes, laminating, researching coins, reading, but no more Amazon shopping! That's gotten out of hand. I've become an online shopping junkie. I've spent maybe $2,000 or even close to $3,000 in the last year. Excessive by any standards. I'm also removing my clock from the bedside table. Worrying about the amount of sleep I'm getting hasn't helped. Knowing that lack of sleep can trigger my seizures and, my sleep patterns being so erratic of late, have probably contributed to my recent spate of events. I slept decent last night, waking a couple times to pee. Would have slept longer except for Coco and his desperate need for food. I'm thinking the chamomile tea and hot shower combo is helping and the walk in the sunshine may have contributed as well.

Thank God we're here in Calgary. The amount of sunshine we get versus the gloomy days back in Surrey, COVID, and mom's passing, I'm sure I would have killed myself. The sense of isolation would be far more severe. Knowing family was physically closer, yet unreachable, would add salt to the wound. Being so close to where Mom had been. Walking by Amica where she died, and her old condo, the Community Hospital, and White Spot wouldn't allow the wound to scab over and heal. Being here, I have my memories to draw upon, letting them wash over me, allow the sadness and remembrance of good times to caress my bruised soul. Just over two months from now and a year will have passed. All the 'firsts' gone through. Her birthday, Mother's Day, Christmas, and New Year's.

Journal Entry, January 28, 2021

I hadn't seen Dr. Harper since November. UPLIFT[7] ended just before Christmas. The first one without Mom. The first time I did all the baking without her. No quick texts or phone calls to double check recipes and instructions. I was in it by myself this time and now forever.

The COVID lock downs, no access to massages and gyms but loads of rich, high-fat, sugary foods bundled with very little sleep, I was a time bomb. It was just a matter of when and how bad. I hadn't been listening to Mozart like before, was more into the cello music, thinking it helped me to get to sleep. Guess I was wrong. I'm showering each night and drinking a cup of chamomile and mint tea. The calming effects of a hot shower and tea seem to help. I'm sleeping better, getting into the deep REM cycle needed to awaken refreshed. But I still tire out by late afternoon, nodding off while reading. I look tired. Black circles under my eyes and no energy. I've restarted the FitnessPal to improve my eating habits and hopefully drop the ten pounds I gained from my Christmas baking and take outs. Devon and I are getting out for walks despite the snow and cold temperatures. I've fallen four times in the last month, which added to my anxieties of going out, with or without Dev.

Since the last seizure, I've had bouts of confusion. Like the other day, as we walked to the Safeway in Kensington. A metal statue we've passed multiple times looked new. The lights in my bathroom were brighter, filling the entire space with a white light, making the room appear larger than it was. But the light hadn't changed. And then the appearance of red splotches like tiny dots superimposed itself over everything I looked at, lasting several minutes at a time. It took a full day before it stopped. The last time this happened was back in January 2019.

I wonder if we should bump up the Escitalopram dose? If a higher dose could reduce my anxiety level, maybe help keep a tighter hold on my fragile countenance and possibly reduce the chance of further events.

Journal Entry, January 31, 2021

I've lost my need to write. I am struggling with this second book. Don't even want to write poetry. Am I bottling up emotions again? Trying to ignore the feelings of anxiety and depression I'm slipping towards? I don't know anymore. All I can think of is all the things I can't do. I can't go for a walk without my son or go shopping by myself. I've lost my independence. I'm now a dependent. Devon's now the parent and I am the child. The Linda of today can't do anything alone. My solitude comes by sitting in a different room, taking out the garbage, checking for mail and walking around the corner to a massage appointment.

The seizures, and not knowing which type, the anxiety, and the darkness that creeps in the shadows; swallowing pills–thinking about knives–jumping off balconies–stepping in front of trains. It's all too much. A force is pulling at me, dragging me down into a mire of despair. This version of me is wrong. It doesn't fit with how I used to be. It doesn't belong.

Journal Entry, February 1, 2021

Things look funny these last two or three days. Lights are brighter and rooms seem lighter as with a new pair of glasses where everything is sharper, larger, and more in focus. The space around furniture appears bigger, like the room grew or the furnishings shrunk. And yet, even with this so-called sharper vision, I've been clumsier. Both hands are dropping things or experiencing difficulties picking items up. I can't determine if it's just the lack of sensation, arthritis, or I'm just not paying attention. I've been tired, nodding off while reading or playing games on my phone. But I'm sleeping and eating better than I was over Christmas. We've gotten out for walks more in January versus December. I'm listening to Mozart again. I've seen things out of the corner of my left eye. Coco sitting or laying there, sleeping or cleaning himself. Blankets and pillows have morphed into his shape. It's weird. My left hand is tingly, flaring up and receding like flames in a fire. At least, I'm not hearing things.

Journal Entry, February 2, 2021

A thought dawned on me yesterday. This need to rearrange, purge, organize, is it all part of building my walls? Was it part of my problem? A means of burying my emotions? Running away from memories and places I wanted to hide from? Instead of facing painful memories, I want to pack up and leave them behind. Is that why I moved so often? I'm fifty-five and besides the childhood homes I grew up in, I've bounced from place to place. Why? What am I looking for? What or who am I running from?

Haven't seen Dr. Harper for two months and UPLIFT[7] won't start up again for another two. I can't volunteer at Foothills and haven't seen Dr. McKay yet. And except for having access to the resources I need; I almost feel as lost as I did in BC. If it weren't for COVID, our move here would look and feel so much different. Dev would be in school, working, and making friends. I'd be volunteering at Foothills, visiting the Alexandra Writer's Centre Society for workshops, going up to Red Deer and Grande Prairie. Losing Mom and the sense of isolation wouldn't be as harsh. I can only hope this vaccine will be COVID's Krypto and I'll see a beam of light halfway through the tunnel.

Journal Entry, February 5, 2021

It felt good talking to Dr. Harper yesterday. She and Dr. Samson have such a calming effect on me. It's like talking to old friends. Is it sad that I feel closer to my doctor and colleagues than to anyone else? They, at least, understand the struggles I face and how it isn't just a 'take one day at a time and all will be right in your world—attitude'. The combination of a physical illness and emotional instability is far more challenging to overcome. Just when I think I've tamed the physical, the apprehension and despondency kicks in. It's difficult to avoid both. Possible, maybe, but emotionally and physically draining trying to achieve it. I need regular support and weekly guidance to help me through the days. But it just isn't possible now. The resources aren't there, or they're stretched beyond capacity. COVID has made everything difficult. Jobs, healthcare, living normal day-to-day lives. We're all stuck in a rut, the mud sucking our feet into the ground, swallowing us up.

Journal Entry, February 8, 2021

I tried acupuncture yesterday. I had a few sessions years ago, but it hadn't provided the release I needed. But this time, the tension inside lifted and oozed out of my pores, relaxing me. This time was an unusual experience. It left me in a dreamy state, like after the reflexology sessions.

While massages untangle the knots, reflexology, and acupuncture releases the tortured soul trapped inside me. Maybe if I alternate the three.

Journal Entry, February 11, 2021

I'm tired of COVID. The restrictions, the masks, and hand sanitizer. I hope this vaccine will put a stop to it. Save us from death. I hate the worry and fear that increases the anxiety and depression I struggle with. This virus combined with the seizures is dragging me down. It sucks the light out of me. Don't want my days spent aimlessly floating along. I just want to feel useful, but the longer I remain in this rut, the deeper I'll sink. I still haven't seen Dr. McKay. The demands on her must be overwhelming by those whose need is probably far greater than mine. Those who don't have a Dr. Harper to talk to.

I'm not looking forward to April 1st. The first anniversary since Mom left. I miss her so much. I've needed to talk to her so many times. To wish her a happy Mother's Day, Happy Birthday, Merry Christmas. I sometimes wonder if she had died of COVID if it would've been easier to accept in a way. To go so suddenly with no sign there was anything wrong. No existing condition that made it understandable, at least. The senseless outcome of a general malaise which led to a cardiac arrest makes little sense and is hard for me to accept, harder to cope with the reality. I love you and miss you, mom. I hope you're at peace wherever you are.

I think back to those days growing up. The old neighbourhood. My friend's dad. How it all started with Barbie and Ken. Two innocent young girls naïve about sex, how men and women meld together creating babies. It began with him talking to us, telling his version of the birds and the bees. Then it progressed to show and tell.

Too many terrible memories surface when I wade through those days from long ago. Best kept in the past. They happened. I moved on. Nothing from back then can hurt me. The scars left their mark, but do not define me. I evolved since then. My hide has toughened, faced far greater trials and tribulations than I ever imagined. It's okay to acknowledge the past, what was done, but it doesn't need to consume me. Those events of the past made me who I am today. A fighter.

Journal Entry, February 13, 2021

I may have had a seizure this morning. Brief, lasting only seconds. I was fine when I got up, just a little tired. My head felt like it was spinning, alternating with pressure, like squeezing a zit. It washed over me like a g-force sensation affecting both head and stomach at times coming and going. While eating breakfast, my left hand became heavy and stiff, turning to stone cold but not tingling.

Over the last week or so, I had stabs of pain at the incision site. Milliseconds of searing pain. I figured it was because of the weather. The temperature dropped, and it snowed on and off, was sunny and cloudy. The rolling sensations this morning stopped and started intermittently, fades for a minute, then starts up again. I was listening to Mozart throughout, trying to focus on the music, things around me, all the while writing it down, letting my thoughts flow. When that didn't work, I shifted my attention to my butt on the chair and feet on the floor. My neck felt stiff, the muscles tight and I was aware of what was happening.

Journal Entry, February 15, 2021

It happened again. The head rush sensation and my left hand felt extremely cold, colder than the right. This time, there was pressure on the right side of my head, like it was caving in. The corner of my mouth drooped. My vision, especially the right eye, was blurry like I smudged my glasses in the centre. I thought I was slipping away, losing consciousness. I did my mindfulness exercises. Breathing, focusing on the Mozart playing through the headphones, feeling my butt on the cushion and my feet on the ottoman. No twitching. Just like the last one, it happened in the morning before I ate breakfast, and before pill time. This time it was more constant and lasted for thirty minutes. I was reading and listening to music. Was aware throughout. A functional seizure, most likely, but I didn't panic and kept it from escalating.

Journal Entry, February 21, 2021

I'm reading the book *Epilepsy Explained. A book for people who want to know more*, by Markus Reuber, MD, Steven C. Schacter, MD, Christian E. Elger, MD, and Ulrich Altrup, MD. I wish I'd known about it six years ago. It explains so much and could have helped me in the early days. Not that they withheld any information, the book just explains it so well. No matter, it's a good read even though I'm aware of most of it now. But it makes me wonder. What would my life be like if the first surgery had stopped my seizures? I don't think I would have driven again. The cost savings and health benefits of walking overrode the need. Besides, I never enjoyed driving, only did it out of need. And I'm not sure I would have gone back to work. No surgery could remove the stress and anxiety from the seizures. Those would always remain a part of who I've become.

I could have volunteered, though. Maybe gained the courage to take transit outside of the three-square miles I lived in. I wouldn't have hired a cleaner. I wouldn't have moved to Calgary. It wouldn't have been necessary. But with FND[2] I wouldn't get the support I do here. My writing wouldn't have developed. *Battles of The Mind* not written, and this one not started. No UPLIFT[7], no Drs. Ingals, Harper, or Samson. I lost so much to get where I am but have gained so much more. My life hasn't been easy. The trials, good and bad, and the wrong decisions which brought me to Calgary. All the ruts in the road, the cracks, twists, and turns were to bring me here. To share my experiences, provide empathy, support, and hope to others like me isolated by an illness that's taken over our lives, destroyed our freedom, wreaking havoc on our brains.

Journal Entry, March 5, 2021

My hand isn't as tingly like it was, and no waves, woozy feelings, or seizures for two weeks. At my appointment with Dr. Harper yesterday, I mentioned my need for ongoing therapy, one-to-one sessions, not a group, massages, Mozart music, and the acupuncture. Explained how much the UPLIFT[7] sessions were helping me. Not just personally, but with helping others. I'm walking more, which helps too. We talked about my limitations and how I'm incapable of living alone. I need help with the basics. The reduced motor skills in both hands limits my ability to tie things, open jars, and grasp items. My balance, poor depth perception, and peripheral issues restrict my activities. Decision making and diminished sense of direction are inconsistent and down the road when Dev moves out, I'll move into independent living like Mom did. Twenty years sooner than I want. My life is mirroring hers in a lot of ways. Widowed, not interested in relationships, or travelling, and frustrated by the limitations of our bodies.

Journal Entry, March 6, 2021

Six years since it all started, really started. Six years, five surgeries, countless seizures, and trips to the emergency room. Twenty thousand dollars spent on care, moving, an FND[2] diagnosis, and pandemic. A lot to go through, almost too much at times and Mom isn't here. My son is now the rock I cling to. Don't know what I'd do without him. I love Alberta, the people, the sunshine and, yes, even the cold and snow. I don't miss BC, the rain, and endless days of grey skies. I may have been born there and my ashes will be next to Mom's, but I won't die there.

Journal Entry, March 12, 2021

I did it! I went to Safeway and back by myself! Dev had gone to the Orthodontist, so I returned to an empty apartment. I was on my own for about two hours, a major achievement. It's the small things that give us the most joy.

Journal Entry, March 21, 2021

Eleven days and it'll be a year since Mom died. Unimaginable. Unreal. Time has slipped away but remains frozen too. The days just come and go, blending into one big blob, suffocating the life out of everyone and everything. Thank God we're here where the sun shines and rain is a thing of the past, plausible but not likely to happen. Snow has taken its place and the cold temperatures. A dry ice effect versus the bone chilling torrent that seeps into your core. I don't miss the grey skies, the wet, dreary days. Of packing umbrellas, slicker, wearing boots, and layers to keep out the damp. I'd rather be cold than feel like a sodden wet rag.

I think I forgot my Friday evening pills. They were in the pillbox when I went to take this morning's meds. That would explain why I felt 'off' yesterday. Not a seizure, but not feeling 'normal'. I put it down to not eating well, the fluctuating weather, and allergy season. Today should be better. I took all my meds yesterday, and I slept well. It's cooler today so that'll help.

Journal Entry, March 22, 2021

I may have had a seizure this morning. Dev and I aren't sure. I was awake early, about 5am and up by 6:30am. We walked twenty-five minutes to his appointment. I bought a Starbucks coffee, read some of my book, and got bus tickets. On our way back, I felt a wave but without the rising. Was dopey, the left side heavy, and I had to sit down. At one point, it was as if my head was closing in, like tunnel vision. We sat for a few minutes, and I focused on the surrounding sounds. There was no shaking. Dev said I looked out of it, but my speech was normal. Eventually, we headed home.

Journal Entry, March 23, 2021

I'm not sleeping well again. Weather related, I keep telling myself, but it's more than that. In nine days, it'll be a year since Mom died. I've never felt so lonely. Mom was a huge part of my life. We were like bosom buddies complaining about our aches and pains, stuck in our small worlds of tv shows, sports, and books. Neither of us had many friends, didn't socialize often, didn't go away, couldn't or didn't drive. Stuck in our own ruts made by choice or some outside influence. It's been a rough year.

Mom going, COVID, seizures, the volunteering at Foothills, and Devon's schooling all on hold.

In five months, we'll have been here for two years. Feels like forever. There's been a few bright spots, but no rainbows. I'm struggling with this book. There's no structure or flow. Just random bits here and there. The upcoming months are going to be challenging. Our next UPLIFT[7] group won't start until the fall. No weekly sessions to look forward to. No interaction and sharing with others like me. I'm going to miss it. I'll need to find something to fill the void once Dev starts school in May. Something other than crossword puzzles, solitaire games, and Amazon shopping.

Journal Entry, March 25, 2021

I'm slowly making a new life here. I have all my doctors in place, connected with the Epilepsy Association of Calgary (EAC), and I have others I can talk to who can relate. Dev will start school in less than two months and will hopefully meet new people. I am concerned how I'll manage the next five to six months without the UPLIFT[7] program. I'm seeing a chiropractor, started acupuncture, and will alternate the reflexology with massage.

Saw the specialist at the Rockyview eye clinic yesterday. The left eye muscles have weakened since last time and we're trying a temporary prism on my glasses to correct the double vision. The next month will be interesting to see how it works out. I think I'll get progressives if proceeding with the prisms. It's probably the best route to go. The eye muscles will only continue to deteriorate, prisms will be my only option at some point.

It snowed overnight and expected to carry on later this morning. Guess Mother Nature didn't get the memo that it was spring. Oh well. The snow doesn't bother me here like it did back in BC. Living downtown has a lot to do with it. Cleared sidewalks and roadways make getting around easier.

I've not been sleeping well again. Waking early. Probably because the one-year anniversary of mom's death is approaching. I can't believe how the time has passed. The days, weeks, and months were a blur. Turbulent emotions, thoughts of suicide, loneliness, anger, and grief. All combined with the fear and depression created by our imposed isolation. Life hadn't stopped just for mom; it stalled for everyone. We're caught in a mini tornado, like the ones you find on a windy day. A swirling mass of dry leaves twirling round and round, going nowhere. And when the air settles, they drop, laying discarded on empty roads, up against curbs, in gutters, covering lawns, roofs, and cars.

Miss you, mom. I feel deserted, left to fend for myself. I thought I had more years. It's all gone now. There isn't anyone left to share your secrets. All that remains are photos, pictures of people I don't know. But I'm glad I have the family archives. That I can glance around the apartment and see and feel you, use your measuring cups, coffee mugs, and double boiler. All things, yes, but covered with your essence. I can feel you, see you when I touch them. They keep you close.

Journal Entry, March 27, 2021

I'm tired. Too much going on this week, and I feel it. Sleep hasn't been the best, despite my efforts to relax before going to bed. A cat who won't let me sleep in doesn't help. The weather too has played a part. Sunny and warm one day, the next minus temperatures and snow, then back again. I want to put my chairs out on the balcony but no point till next month.

No energy today. I'm not going anywhere. This week is a lighter load. Reflexology tomorrow, acupuncture Tuesday, Dr. Harper Thursday, and chiropractor Friday. And the following week, I only have two appointments. For now. I have lots of 'projects' that will help keep me busy. Finish this next book, rewrite my older poems, organize and value the coins etc. There's lots to occupy myself in the upcoming months until UPLIFT[7] starts in the fall. Who knows, by year's end I could volunteer at the hospital or with the Epilepsy Association of Calgary. Lots of possibilities. I don't believe I'm in this situation for no reason. I have a job to do, a role to fill. Exactly what that is or isn't, is unknown, but involves the need to help others like me. To support them and help them get through the dark times.

Journal Entry, March 30, 2021

I wanted to hurt myself, to see a scar, to see blood and know it's real that it has substance and not just in my mind.

Here I am again on the eleventh floor. Seizure yesterday in the Circle K, taken to the emergency, then up to Unit 111. They kept me overnight. It happened so fast.

We walked only two or three blocks. The wind was strong and cold like brain freeze on the forehead. We got our drinks paid and turned to leave. I remember an enormous wave of sensation, was lightheaded, became weak and fell to the floor. I recall bits and pieces. Someone rolled me onto my side and glasses removed. Voices. Devon's. I'm not sure when the shaking began. Breathing hard, I couldn't get my breath. A vague memory of being lifted, then nothing.

I don't know what time it was when I came to in the emergency room or when they brought me up to 111. I think I started seizing again in emergency, and they loaded me up with Dilantin. My left side is weak, my hand tingly. I'm dopey, tired, and sad. I tried to cut my wrist with a plastic knife! How pathetic is that?! I called the nurse, and she took my tray away. Tears flowed, alternating between trickling and streams. I have pains on the right side of my head. My mouth feels droopy on the left. I'm a mess emotionally and physically.

Maybe being at Foothills gave me what I need to get through tomorrow. Get through the worst part. I think the emotional torrent would have been difficult for Devon to handle. I have Dr. Harper in the morning and the rest of the day to curl into a ball until my massage on Tuesday. Mustn't blame myself or get discouraged about this last event. The anniversary of mom's death and not sleeping well contributed to the stress and resulting seizure. Those and my eyes. I must contact the eye doctor and get those progressive lenses. I was going to proceed with prisms and now that I don't have an enormous tax bill, there's no need to stress over the cost.

How does my body feel? Head pressure, on the right side, the odd flare of pain, heavy, and a headache. Eyes dry, heavy, achy, shoulders stiff and neck tight. My arms are weak, the left forearm plus the hand tingles. Stomach relaxed and hungry. Legs weak, left foot tingly, warm, and heavy. I feel sleepy. I guess this was a big one that knocked the stuffing out of me.

It's amazing how one can pass the time without technology, at least for those of us born before 1980. Doodling, adding up random numbers, writing out the alphabet, coming up with words for each letter. I've printed for so long now I've forgotten how to write in cursive form. Maybe that's an exercise I can do while listening to music. An activity that requires some focus without the use of technology, well other than a pen. I need to find more things to occupy my mind. Activities to stop the thoughts and worries of having seizures and not knowing which one it was. My concern over losing my vision, frustration over my hand and the resulting anger. No matter what I do, meditation, mindfulness techniques, exercise, these constant thoughts won't leave me. Hopefully, by sitting out on the balcony in a warm breeze and watching the traffic and trains will provide another distraction and calm the noise. A perfect setting to sit, listen, and see, allowing the senses to enter my being, easing my tension.

Journal Entry, March 31, 2021

I didn't finish my poem, Mom. I've been so focused on writing my book that poetry and journaling were nonexistent dribs and drabs written in fits and starts. Mere tidbits of what lurks inside. Am I hiding again? Burying my emotions behind yet another wall I've created? Maybe. I'm just so tired of it all. The seizures, the hospitals, and ambulances, doctor appointments, and tests. Sick and tired of washing masks, using hand sanitizer, and the restrictions on where I can go. I suppose if I can get through COVID, Mom dying, the seizures, my depression, and thoughts of hurting myself, I can get through anything.

Journal Entry, April 4, 2021

A good session with Dr. Harper the other day. She always makes me feel better. Guess it's getting all the emotions out that lightens my soul. She suggested re-reading *Living Like You Mean It: Use the Wisdom and Power of Your Emotions to Get the Life You Really Want* and allow myself to feel. My childhood stunted my emotional growth. My overbearing father and my friend's dad all helped to develop the walls I've built to protect me. To keep those awful memories from escaping limiting their power over me.

Journal Entry, April 5, 2021

Emotionally immature and impaired by an upbringing without feeling left me ill-equipped to handle what life has thrown at me. The terrible relationships, and the verbal and sexual abuse suffered as a child, had left me vulnerable. A prime candidate for FND[2].

But not until my epilepsy and functional seizure diagnoses did I realize to what extent my childhood experiences had on my psyche. How disabled and out of touch with myself I was. Still am. Not sure what being in love is. Mistaken acceptance and companionship as love. Never popular or sought after, I was just a body that filled a void. Spent my life on a self-improvement path constantly looking for approval. I lacked the self confidence to put myself out there assert myself, and articulate what I wanted, placing the needs of others ahead of mine. I'm uncomfortable in the spotlight, can't handle the attention without feeling inferior. I've become empty, a shell of flesh and bone lifeless and unfeeling. Numb.

Journal Entry, April 11, 2021

Writing about my childhood has been good. It's brought old forgotten memories to the surface that should have been dissected years ago. The paperboy who'd felt me up and the embarrassment of telling my parents and talking to the police. I have a vague picture of standing on the patio next to my dad. A cop was there, and I had to tell them what happened. How he touched my chest, rubbing the area where puberty hadn't quite reached. Looking back as an adult with the knowledge and awareness available today, there wasn't any help for that scared little girl to exorcise the pain of those events. No guidance to show her how to tap into those feelings, acknowledge them, and recognize she wasn't at fault. No need to hide those emotions and, in fact, shouldn't be. By not reconciling the past and acknowledging what occurred, it's no wonder I'm not tuned into my emotions and how they festered within my body. You can't know what you don't know.

Journal Entry, April 14, 2021

This move to Calgary is my chance to sever the emotional ties of the past. To be 'me' in my own right. Be my own person, not the daughter of or a sister of, just Linda. Here, I was a patient, a volunteer, a donor. I was assessed on what people saw and experienced from me. Not by an older sibling or parent. I'm known here, not my family. My history started in 2016, not at birth. They can't compare me to anyone not even myself, the person I had been.

Journal Entry, April 16, 2021

I'm getting my COVID vaccine today. Am I worried? Yes, and no. How quickly they pushed it through without the usual red tape, is disarming, but considering this pandemic has imprisoned us for the last year, it's worth it; I think. This extra layer of protection besides social distancing, masks, hand washing and sanitizing will ease my mind slightly. Possibly reduce my anxiety over it and causing more seizures than I've already experienced. It all circles back to my seizures, doesn't it? Whether this or that will trigger them, if it's an epileptic one or not. The toll on my body and mind has been tremendous, far more than if I only had one or the other. Combined with vision issues, mom's passing, and COVID, it's no wonder my mood has deteriorated, that I wanted to hurt myself while in hospital. And that is why I reached out to the Epilepsy Association of Calgary to complement my sessions with Dr. Harper. I feel like Job, beset with trials and tribulations meant to crush me, testing my strength and faith in myself to persevere. To get up, dust myself off, and keep trudging along looking for that silver lining, they say every dark cloud has; grasping to the belief that everything happens for a reason and God only dishes out what he knows you can handle. Believing there are others worse off and to stop feeling sorry for yourself. But that's the problem, or part of it. Not feeling, ignoring the pain inside, trapping it in a corner and stomping on it and killing it before it can take hold.

Journal Entry, April 26, 2021

Digging through the layers of rotting emotions opened my mind, and I learned a lot about myself. The constant feelings of inadequacies and not belonging, have been with me since my earliest recollection. Feeling insignificant, my thoughts and opinions pushed aside. I didn't fit anywhere. Sat on the edge looking in, flitted from one group to another at school, settling briefly before moving on. A butterfly, a bee, in search of nectar, not finding enough to sustain my hunger. I sought attention, but not the healthy kind. I didn't know any better. Gut reactions telling me there's danger, informing me to fight or flee, were stifled, malfunctioned, and broken. My choices in men were copies of myself. The opposite gender carrying their own suitcases and trunks of hidden feelings, unsure whether to toss, store, or display. I was a threat to the tight security they'd placed around their emotions, and they struck out in defence. Wrapping themselves in alcohol and drugs to stay numb, pushing me closer to the edge, wanting and waiting for my eventual surrender, following them into the dark. Knowing myself better now, having cracked the window to see what's inside, I know not to fall into the same trap. Not allow my impaired judgement to cause the same mistakes. I don't know right or wrong or what's best in relationships. No matter how lonely it may seem, I'm better off getting to know 'me'. The one that's hidden behind walls, placed into boxes and put on shelves. The caterpillar has cocooned for far too long. It's time to break through my casing, unfurl my wings and fly.

Journal Entry, May 2, 2021

So that's been a week! Symptoms of COVID sent me to the hospital on Thursday, one month to the day since my last visit. And, of course, since I'm there, let's have a seizure or three. Fuck my life!! Good news is I don't have pneumonia or COVID. A cold? Allergies? The dry air? A combo? No matter. I'm home, slowly getting better. They loaded me up on Dilantin while in emergency, Dr. Young's orders. So not a functional seizure then? Or, as a precaution? I'll find out Wednesday at our appointment. I finished my spreadsheet, just need to tweak it and print. Will be easier for me to compare each year on paper versus screen. This year hasn't started out as well as I'd hoped. Better, but not. I haven't had as many seizures thus far, and yet there's been more trips to the emergency. But on the flip side, I've made some progress. Memories from childhood have surfaced. Events stuffed into the nook and crannies of my subconscious buried away and forgotten. It's been good to talk about them, share them. It's good for Dev to know and give him insight into how I am, what makes me tick and understand why I do what I do.

Journal Entry, May 4, 2021

I can feel my mood slipping, sliding into that funky space in my head where daylight becomes murky, and the energy depletes. I don't feel like doing anything. Even getting dressed is a chore, the thoughts of 'why bother? I can't go anywhere. I am getting better, but this forced isolation is depressing. It dampens the spirit, weighing it down. Its once light and airy mood crushed. I should be used to the confines of a cell, locked away in a nine-by-nine room. It isn't anything new except the location. It's harder to accept when trapped within your own home other than a hospital. You can feel life moving out there without you.

Journal Entry, May 11, 2021

The sense of isolation presses in on me, holding me down, engulfing me in loneliness and despair, without any tender arms, soft hands or soothing voice to comfort me. A bubble surrounds me, a thick membrane unyielding, impervious to any pointed object looking to puncture it. Silence roars, filling my ears, echoing inside my head and throughout my body. Vibrating, pulsating, shocking the nerves into action. Anxiety increases the feeling of doom and suspense; the calm before all hell breaks loose ripping me apart.

Journal Entry, May 13, 2021

I think the weather is mucking up my head. The pressure fluctuations are creating a dizzy like sensation. A swirling mass inside buffeting my brain and twirling upward like the helicopter bits from trees spinning rapidly as they fall to the ground. It's the Chinook curse. When a Chinook blows in during the winter a temperature of minus twenty degrees Celsius can shoot upwards to minus five degrees Celsius in a matter of hours or days and, just as suddenly, plummet back down. Not a pleasant situation for one susceptible to headaches like me.

Lately I'm plagued by thoughts of, is a seizure starting? What's my body doing? Is that a sign of COVID? Am I losing my sight? Will I ever be able to live alone? Should I get a cane? If I must, will that mean I can't run on the treadmill? A constant eddy of Will I? Can I? What if? All stupid questions that have no answers in the present. The future will unfold as it always does, whether I'm prepared for the outcome or not. I keep reminding myself I can't change the past, should focus on today and hold on as the future pulls me forward.

Journal Entry, May 16, 2021

I'm experiencing similar feelings like I had back in 2014 and 2015. Sensations in my stomach that I thought were from a weird flu bug, only to discover they were focal aware seizures. Not the stronger ones I labelled as anxious wavy feelings. They're milder, more like the beginnings of a wave or the ripples a stone makes when tossed into a pond. Anxiety perhaps? A functional seizure? Epileptic seizure? I just don't know anymore. It's a guessing game and not just a single player one. Dev isn't sure, can't even hazard a guess. Me? I want it to be my epilepsy but try to tell myself they're FND[2]. But I always lean towards the tangible, the physical proof and shy away from what I can't see. One of my dad's beliefs. Believe nothing of what you hear, and only half of what you see. But what if you can't see it? Does it exist only because you can feel it, hold it, mold it into a shape? What then about oxygen? You can't see it, touch it, taste it, hear it and yet it's real because we exist.

    The complexities of my brain and its inner workings are a challenge. Despite the abnormalities shown on scans, the reality escapes me. Even more so, the concept of mind over matter and the hijacking of my body. How my emotions, held at bay, and buried at sea, have escaped. The evolution of time altered their form and created a tsunami. An onslaught of memories full of pain, sorrow, grief, and anger overwhelming the conscious state. Why wasn't counselling, CBT, mindfulness, stress reducing techniques talked about earlier? Depression and anxiety are well-known effects of epilepsy, the degree of which causes some to take their lives, ending their misery. Why must the situation reach the point where turning back is almost not possible? There just aren't the resources out there, in BC at least, and not enough here in Alberta to treat everyone. Thank God for Foothills and the Epilepsy Clinic. The doctors, surgeons, nurses, and techs, such a diverse group of caring individuals with a common goal. To help others like me, keeping us safe, finding solutions and the strength to fight.

We're cleaning the balcony today. Washing the deck, railings, and windows. It's mid-May and I want my chairs set up. I want to relax outside in the warm air with my morning coffee and meditate, write or read, and watch the world below and escape.

Journal Entry, May 19, 2021

Words have left me. I sit staring at a blank page, a mirror image of my mind an empty wasteland of nothing. I struggle to conjure up thoughts to share but I'm hollow, the silence echoes within, consumed by a body that's becoming more useless each day. A short-circuited brain, hands no longer nimble an eye turning inwards losing sight of the big picture, the scenery blurred, doubled almost beyond recognition. The world is muffled, the sounds distorted, a rumbling mass of noise. The right side in pain, the left is numb, two parts of a body at war pulling itself apart.

Journal Entry, May 27, 2021

I'm not unique in the epilepsy world, just unusual, a mystery, an enigma. Being different increases the sense of isolation. I have yet to connect with anyone like me. Others who are drug resistant, diagnosed later in life, and scarred by surgery, depressed and anxious, and living with two seizure disorders. I've met surgical cases, but theirs were successful. Met others whose medications won't control their seizures, but none who are so depressed and anxious they struggle with suicidal thoughts and ideations. I know of others with both disorders, but none which included surgery.

I'm meeting Dr. McKay today at Foothills. I haven't been up to the twelfth floor in months. Not since Dr. Ingals' follow up October 19, 2020, seven months ago! Wow! Where did all that time go? The days, weeks, months, disappeared and the only trace are calendar entries to confirm they were real.

Journal Entry, June 2, 2021

Aah. The balcony is done. The deck cleaned rugs down and furniture placed. With Mozart playing, a book, or journal and a mug of coffee, my day begins. The sun peaks through filmy clouds, plays hide and seek behind office towers, a beautiful way to start the day in tune with my body. The steady hum of engines in the background, moving people and cargo this way and that, stop and go, back and forth busy as ants returning to the nest. An endless stream of life in the here and now.

I can't believe June is almost over. Six months gone. Eighteen months of this COVID, so many lives lost, others destroyed by cutbacks, isolation, and depression. Survived the loneliness of a new home in a new city. Plans of school, work, volunteering, and new friends are an illusion of the mind imprisoned by an invisible bug, lethal and frightening.

Journal Entry, June 7, 2021, Foothills Medical Centre Emergency Department

I came to slowly, head bursting as my right temple throbbed. I knew I had a seizure, that Dev called 911, but what time was it? How long have I been here? I was shaving my head over the bathroom sink, my mind playing over different routes to take to complete my errands. A slight wave, some nausea, and shaky limbs interrupted my musings. Breathe Linda, just breathe. In, out, in, out, slow, and steady. Count the swipes of the razor. One, two, front to back, listen to the buzz: one, two, one, two. In, out, big breath in, blow it out. Okay, let's check our progress. Standing, leaning against the counter, my head slowly lifted, my eyes watching the mirror. Woozy, dizzy, whoa! My body fell. Dev! Help! I fell backwards. I thought I hit the wall behind me. Then darkness.

Five hours later, groggy, and sore, thirsty, head pounding with Dilantin pumping into my veins.

"Hello Ms. McClure, how are you feeling? It seems your Dilantin levels are low. Have you missed a dose?"

"No. They're always below therapeutic range. No pills missed. I have them in blister packs and two alarms."

"Hmph, maybe you should look to increase your dose…"

"No, my epileptologist doesn't want to increase my meds. I'd been toxic before. My dosage stays the same."

"And your neurologist is Dr. Young, yes?"

"Yes."

"Ok well, we've run some bloodwork, and everything looks good. No usual indications of an epileptic event. So, I'm thinking this was one of your, one of, a pseudo seizure." I glared at him. The hairs on my head bristled, lips tightened, eyes narrowed.

"Don't you call them that! They're not pseudo seizures!" His hands raised placatingly, he stepped back, surprised.

"Yes, well, um, you know one of those, um, psy, those non-epilep…"

"Psychogenic non-epileptic seizures[1]."

"Yes, those."

"Don't you ever call them pseudo seizures. They're real!" The words came out clipped, precisely intent on driving my point into his thick head.

"Right, well, once you're up to it, you can go. Let the nurse know when you're ready."

I'd heard of other patients being spoken to like that, heard tales of the lack of care and empathy by medical professionals who should know better. Up until then, I hadn't had the pleasure. Did that mean every doctor, nurse, EMT, and paramedic I've encountered were fully aware of FND[2]? Probably not, but they knew better than to treat patients obviously in distress without some amount of empathy, kindness, and dignity.

Journal Entry, June 9, 2021

Thoughts of 'will this ever end? Why me? How much more can I take?' have returned and I hate what it's doing to me. This melancholy state I've fallen into, the fear, anger, hopelessness, and feeling helpless that nothing I do will make things better. My life will continue to rotate on the hamster wheel going round and round, getting nowhere. I'm stuck in a circle where only brief moments of light shine through the thin slats I cling to as it rolls me in this pile of manure.

The seizure on Monday had to be the first where I ended up injured. The goose egg on my head confirms Dev's suspicion that I'd hit it when I fell. I recall feeling wavy and nauseous as I leaned over the bathroom sink, shaving my head. As the feelings struck, I focused on the buzz of the shaver and counted the strokes as it passed over my head, depositing tufts of hair into the garbage bag placed strategically to catch the clumps. The wavy sensations kept building, becoming waves washing over me like tiny shocks of electricity coursing through every nerve. My memory is fuzzy after I straightened up to check my progress in the mirror. I'm not sure what I did. Only recall falling, or the sense of falling, and hearing a bang. Voices faded in and out, sounding far away as if deep in a valley through a tunnel. It seemed as if I was dreaming, locked away in another world held back by a wall which I couldn't penetrate. The next thing I remember is breathing heavily, spit accumulating in my mouth bubbling out as I pushed air from my lungs. Then breathing became difficult. I couldn't get enough air to fill my lungs and I panicked; I think. Vaguely recall saying I couldn't breathe over and over. Help me make it stop. My neck must have been strained, the muscles on the right side still hurt today. It wasn't until I got up yesterday; I discovered I'd bitten my tongue. Not a chewed up indistinguishable lump like it was back in 2011, just a single indent grooved into the left side from a molar. Tender to touch it made eating a challenge. As per usual, my vision on the left side restricted, more so than it had been recently. It was as though I had a stroke. The left side almost useless. Days prior to the event, I'd experienced waves, sharp pains above the right eye. I told myself it was weather related. Thunderstorms had blown in and out, the pressure building and falling. I blamed the new anti-depressant I was on for the periodic bouts of nausea, but inside, I was stressed about my eyes, the nerve deterioration, double vision, and pulling together my book proposal. All these pieces of my life hovered in my thoughts like sugarplums dancing in my head, but sour, not the sweet treats that melt in your mouth.

Journal Entry, June 12, 2021

Another month and a half gone and nothing to show for it, other than a trip to the emergency department. That's the third time this year. At $385 a pop, I'm more than covering the gas to get me there. Getting my second vaccine dose on Monday. Just in time for when they open things up again.

Heh, what a welcome to our new home, eh? Two years come August and isolated from the world. A tighter cocoon in a different location, sheltering me from life. Maybe I'll be able to volunteer at Foothills next year. I've been thinking a lot about what my future will look like once Dev gets his own place. I know it's a futile exercise, too many unknown variables and missing parts to even make an educated guess. Like, when will the functional seizures go away? Will I ever get control of my epilepsy? It's too soon to look at options and it only stresses me further. I need to focus on today, looking no further than tomorrow or the week ahead and what appointments or activities I have. I need to finish my book proposal, schedule time to work on book number two and, once it reopens, get back to the gym. Relieving my stress and the tension in my body with exercise will relax me and reduce the seizures. My mood will improve and burning calories and toning muscles, will alleviate my worries over my weight.

It feels so weird not having Mom here. She was my sounding board, confidante, my best friend. I miss the private jokes, watching *As Time Goes By* with her, our Xmas Bake-a-thons, talking about books, tv shows, hockey. I feel deflated, empty, alone, and miss the fun times. I miss her but I'm thankful she's not around to deal with COVID. She'd have worried herself to death if she'd been here. She'd have stressed over the numbers increasing there and here in Alberta. Her stress levels would've been through the roof, increasing her blood pressure, placing a strain on her body and mind. As much as I'd love her to still be here, it was for the best. She's at peace, and that's what really matters.

Journal Entry, June 20, 2021

My first morning sitting on my balcony in the sun wearing my new glasses. I'm still adjusting to them. The bifocal lenses are so different from any I've had before. The last time I saw both near and far with any clarity was before my eye surgery in 2006. My double vision tamed, for now, and with transition lenses, the need for sunglasses removed. This and the gym reopening plus the whole of Alberta on July 1st is a lovely way to start the summer. Maybe 2020 was my transition year. A time to mourn not just the loss of Mom but leaving my home to start fresh, morph into someone new and become my own person with no preconceived notions of who I am.

I love my new home, my doctors, landlords. Everyone I've encountered has been so open and welcoming. My army of doctors and health professionals has multiplied. My whole body and mind are being cared for. I feel blessed, happy; I think. Hopeful maybe.

Journal Entry, June 25, 2021

2020 was a transition year I'm sure of it now. It was an intense time of isolation bringing Dev and me closer than before. We supported each other; him caring for me versus the other way round. He's grown into a man, takes his role of looking out for his momma seriously, managing my seizures on his own. We're good roommates. Enjoy each other's company, a few laughs, and have our own interests which allow each of us 'me' time, lost in our own worlds. I guess I did something right. I raised a great kid. Smart, generous, funny, and loving. Couldn't ask for a better son.

I can't believe I live in downtown Calgary and love it! Traffic flows around us, a constant hum of tires and engines, sirens, and train horns. Compared to the quiet stillness of the townhouse, the noise is deafening but comforting in a time of fear, isolation, and death. The movement of life is reassuring. Others still exist. We're not alone, we have survived.

Journal Entry, July 4, 2021

Mom used to say I was more Virgo than Leo. Where a Leo is considered promiscuous, a Virgo is reserved. Leos are flamboyant, crave the spotlight. Virgos prefer to work behind the scenes, planning, tweaking, and controlling the outcome. They are quiet, intelligent folk, generous and nurturing, a safe port in the storm. Leos are the life of the party, gregarious and entertaining. I'm no Leo. I prefer the shadows, the anonymity of self, mostly quiet, I prefer to watch and listen, unsure of my capabilities to take part. I like order, not spontaneity. Organized schedules laid out well in advance, an answer to the five W's. Where, what, who, when, and why? It's all about control and a sense of comfort. My life and my rules, not someone else's. Doing what comes easily, no pressure to perform based on another's expectations, answering only to myself. In the end, it's always about control no matter who you are in the big scheme of things.

Journal Entry, July 9, 2021

Wow, what a month! I reached out to the volunteer services at Foothills, and they've reopened the eleventh floor! Yay! Yay! New police check and my final onboarding tour and I'm ready to go. Finally! It's the start of great things. Volunteering one day a week at Foothills, the eight weekly sessions of UPLIFT[7], and possibly Peer to Peer, maybe? I must make time for myself, my writing and the gym in addition to doctors appointments, massages, acupuncture, and reflexology. I mustn't overdo things and may need to scale back now and again. I'm getting ahead of myself again planning out a future I don't know yet. I may only have time and energy for Foothills and appointments, plus the gym. We'll see. Just sit back and relax, take one day at a time.

Journal Entry, July 17, 2021

Saw the ophthalmologist yesterday. The eye pressure from the glaucoma is down, the nerve is stable, and no change to the peripheral. Guess I won't be going blind today.

I'm waiting for the police check and training modules before I can start volunteering. Dev registered for his next course at SAIT and is doing well so far. We're both vaccinated. Dev is managing well with his braces and Mom's estate is almost done. COVID is receding like the tide, slow but definite. The gym is back open and usually empty when we arrive. Between that and my massage treatments, the stress appears to be under control. Life is good right now. My only 'issues', the seizures, and my ear, nose, and throat but even those are being dealt with. Dev is twenty-seven tomorrow. My little baby boy now a grown man. Twenty-one inches. Sprouted to six foot three. A gentle giant with a big heart and strong limbs. I don't know what I'd do without him.

I have no desire to go back to BC. I'm a prairie girl now. Traded sandy beaches, oceans, and majestic mountains for rivers and foothills, sunny skies, and little to no rain. The damp air and ocean breezes turned to minus thirty with dry icy winds. Snow and sun replaced the dull grey and wet. People here seem more down to earth, family oriented, and neighbour friendly. Must be the sunshine, and fewer bodies in wide open spaces. My transition to Cowtown, even in downtown, has surprised me. Twenty storeys up amid tall towers, squat buildings, trains, and trams. I've found my Oasis, a shelter from the storms. I love it here. This is home.

Journal Entry, August 1, 2021

Another month is over. Heat warning today, the smoke is oppressive, heavier than it would be otherwise. Eight weeks since my last event on June 7th. Made it through July seizure free. I volunteer this month. My first two shifts I'll be shadowing another volunteer. Neurology and stroke patients. I'm looking forward to it. It's been too long in the making, delayed by over a year. Another casualty thanks to COVID.

Journal Entry, August 6, 2021

So tired this week. My first volunteer shift. Four hours followed by a poetry class and I'm knackered. Then, two days later, a return trip to Foothills to see Dr. Harper. Now nothing until Sunday and reflexology. Next week shouldn't be as bad. Another shadow shift Tuesday night, and a class on Thursday night. The rest of the month is light until we sort out my volunteer shifts. One day a week is plenty. I couldn't do more than that. Mornings would be best. I'm tired by mid afternoons and useless at night. It felt good to do what I'd aimed to do after moving here. To give back to all those who helped me, pay it forward, empathize with those going through all the same things I have, multiple times. It gives me the sense of purpose I've needed since the beginning of all this.

I've reached four months of seizure freedom before, I'm halfway there now. Two months and counting. My biggest concern is sleep. An average of five to six hours per night isn't enough. And Coco doesn't help. This morning, he woke me at 6:30 am. Walking over my stomach, poking his face into mine, knocking my phone off its stand, caterwauling and carrying on. Petting him and scratching his neck and ears hadn't placated him and I had to get up. Once up, I couldn't get back to sleep. I've always been that way. Insufficient sleep triggers my seizures and has a negative impact on my moods. Having the two seizure disorders makes it all the more imperative to get a good night's rest.

Journal Entry, August 12, 2021

I'm really struggling with this second book. It's hard to find a beginning, middle and end. I must remember I'm not just writing about FND^2; it's about having FND^2 with seizures and epilepsy and the struggles of living with both. I guess it will be mostly my journal entries and details of the seizures themselves. Not so much about the interactions with family, friends, or doctors. It's the inner battles, how the mind plays games and takes over physically and mentally. How the trauma of the last six years contributed to the development of FND^2. Uncovering the source brought back long forgotten memories and emotions I buried deep. All those years of feeling inadequate, unimportant, lacking any confidence, shying away from confrontation, were the catalysts to erecting my walls. I spent my teen years wandering from group to group, searching for that keyhole to unlock my cage and set me free. It was easier to orbit on the fringe, less chance of getting hurt, or manipulated. To isolate and be a loner was better than being shunned. Rummaging through this trunk full of keepsakes, ones that I should have tossed, burned, and shredded years ago, made me see how immature my emotional being was, and still is. If you're not taught how to perform a task, how would you know? You couldn't.

And after decades of tossing away useless crap, letting it pile up and building my walls so it wouldn't ooze out, it finally crumpled. The dam broke, cracking in the centre after the first seizure. Then after the second, the first few bricks fell away. Then by the third, a whole side had blown. As the neurons fired, the brick and mortar crumbled, leaving gaps and the crap leaked out. By the time three years had passed, the fortress was gone. Only a brick or two remained, the only clue that something once stood there. And then the games began. Multiple seizures the same yet different, just as scary and long, sometimes longer. Coming from a source still buried beneath the rubble, flattened by the weight of time, covered with a layer of cracked mortar, dust, and manure. To sift through each layer, separate truth from fiction, and analyze the results takes time. Such a slow process but necessary to uncover the cause, learn how to deal with it and remove its effects.

Journal Entry, September 12, 2021

Guilt: I know I shouldn't feel it, and yet the sense of disappointment weighs me down. Or maybe it's more like disgust, hating myself for the choices I've made, not recognizing some were out of my control. Guilt is a funny thing. A sense of doing wrong even though it's for the best.

As Dr. Harper said, adults make their own decisions, and I must accept that Devon moving with me to Calgary was his choice, not mine. Staying throughout the turmoil of seizures and hospital trips, watching over me, making sure I'm safe. 'It's his choice to be here', Dr. Harper had said. 'He's an adult and I have no control over his actions and shouldn't feel guilty for what he does or doesn't do'.

But it's hard. I'm his mother. I'm supposed to look after him, teach him to stand on his own, to move on with his life, forge his own path, create a future independent from mine. He shouldn't need to be my caretaker at least, not at our ages. He's only twenty-seven, for Christ's sakes! I shouldn't be a burden at this age. Fifty-six is too early. It should've been much later, like seventy, eighty or God forbid, if I lived until ninety. And yet, I've taught him to be his own person, and decide where he goes and how. I guess it's hypocritical of me not to recognize it and accept his presence, knowing he's not going anywhere.

My penchant to please others and placing their needs before mine is part of my problem, part of why I've hidden behind a façade, as my protection from harm. Not feeling is better than allowing the tides of emotion knock me over and spluttering for air with a mouthful of sand and water. And how has that worked out? Living behind a fortress of rock and steel allowing no one in?

Journal Entry, October 7, 2021

The forced isolation and social restrictions, suits me. A loner never belonging in any one space justifies my anti-socialistic behaviour. Forces me, no allows me to hide behind my walls. No pressure to go out among the masses, accept dinner invitations, coffee dates, or walks. It's okay to stay away. It's the new 'thing', it's fashionable and safe.

My compulsive nature to organize, putting everything in order, has overridden thoughts of seizures, suicide, and self harm. The constant need for change, leaving the negative aspects of my life behind, is a rebirth born by the desire to start fresh, wipe the slate off, and move on. It's my way of taking control, clearing out the clutter and throwing out the trash, widening my view of the world to explore new opportunities. I'm shifting from the past and present to a future filled with promise and new beginnings.

Going way back to my childhood, I've written off those who've hurt me, erected an impenetrable wall around them, shutting them out, permanently deleting them from my spam folder barring them from my life. I shut them all away, stuffing them down into a well of pain, and sealed them off with layers of concrete. Even as Dr. Harper and I chip away at the layers, slowly exposing the forgotten treasures, and worthless ones at that, I've patched up the holes with new emotions, people, and experiences I no longer wish to acknowledge. Some habits are hard to break.

But I have changed, if only slightly. I'm better at acknowledging what my body is saying. Becoming in tune with the grief of Mom leaving, my altered state and recognizing a future filled with limitations. I can express myself, how I feel in a given moment, logically weeding out those anxious riddled emotions, sifting through reality and tossing out the ridiculous thoughts with no basis in truth. I'm getting better at asking for help, knowing my limitations and finding workarounds, listening to my body when it needs rest and spreading tasks over days not just hours. I'm getting there, I'm a work in progress being molded and shaped into a new structure, more stable and stronger.

Journal Entry, November 10, 2021,
Canadian tire seizure*

It happened outside the store. I was trying to put a box on my shopping cart to go home when I became confused, my coordination impaired, lightheaded almost wavy and had to sit. I tried to call Devon but couldn't see the phone icons. I tried asking Google but it didn't work. Everything is foggy from there. I think I asked for help to call him. I think someone rolled me onto my side and removed my headphones. At one point I felt like throwing up and then nothing until I awakened in the emergency room.

Email from Mark [Canadian Tire security]

So, as I discussed with you, I showed you the footage. You were trying to attach a box to your cart and then you stopped and sat down. You pulled out your phone, and you then scooted on your bum. A few mins later you laid down and were crawling toward the edge and then almost to the exit doors. When I approached you, I turned you onto your side and another coworker, Ruby, was rubbing your back. We tried to talk to you, but you were unresponsive. Your body was not moving much, just shaking. Your eyes were open the whole time and were fluttering. You, at one point I think, said you were gonna throw up, but other than that, maybe just grunting sounds coming from you. I stood over you, letting your body lean on my leg to keep you on your side. I then walked away when firefighters showed up.

Dev's impression of Canadian Tire surveillance video

It sounds like all the others I've had. Video shows some similarities but isn't clear except for moving around, crawling on the floor. Normally I'm just sitting, laying there, i.e. stationary other than some twitching.

(NOTE: *We asked for a copy of the store's video surveillance for Dr. Young to review and was denied. Copies of surveillance tapes are only given to the police. Even with a letter from my doctor, they wouldn't release a copy. Store policy).*

Journal Entry, November 19, 2021

Why is it after every seizure I ask myself, 'what did I do wrong? How did I cause it?' Each time I have one, I still assume it was something I did. Whether it was an epileptic or functional seizure, it happened because of a conscious effort on my part to produce it. It wasn't the firing neurons or an emotional response to an outside influence. It was me. It's my fault.

It takes effort to remind myself that these events occur whenever and wherever they want to, and I have no say. That it's nothing I'm doing. As Dr. Young told me, the brain can only handle so much before it snaps. It would not differ from stretching an elastic band beyond what it could handle, and it breaks.

CHAPTER NINE

2022—Weights And Measures—A Balancing Act

Embrace the positive versus negative. Get out in the fresh air and breathe. Believe in your higher power to see you through to the next moment. Reach out to others and make them smile. Take this time to purge and donate unwanted items. With restricted activities, use this opportunity to save your pennies otherwise spent on social activities not available right now. Even white puffy clouds have a silver lining, as with a rainbow after a shower, you must look up and search for it.

Journal Entry, March 27, 2022

Nothing. Silence of space. The emptiness of darkness and blank moments staring without seeing, eyes dull like a cloudy day. Something is wrong. Stumbling through time unaware. The aura of light which outlines the physical has dimmed, flickering as a flame blown by a puff of air. Lost. Going in circles, unsure of the destination. No signs. No directions. A vast gulf of no one, alone by myself. Nothing there. No guiding lights. Staring into a mindless existence with no beginning, no end. No sound, just a heavy weight of nothing.

Journal Entry, April 13, 2022

  I find myself in limbo yet again, wavering between positives and negatives, waiting for appointments, and the possibility of eye surgery to correct my double vision and glaucoma, and the next seizure. Another two weeks to reach that two-month goal of seizure freedom. Something that's been outside of my grasp, always just out of reach. At least the Peer-to-Peer Program[8] is up and running.

  I wish a program like Peer to Peer[8] was around during my visits to the unit. The long, lonely days spent without visitors, only the nurses, technologists, doctors, cleaners, and those who brought my meals to converse with. Confined to a small space, some without windows, no room to manoeuver around hospital beds, attached to a 'leash' long enough to reach a shared washroom and no further. In a way, I'm glad I can share my lived experiences, the trips from another province, the three temporal lobe surgeries, and functional seizure diagnosis. With the complexities of my epilepsy, the treatments, tests, and therapies I can provide the support that no doctor or family member without a seizure disorder can give. The relationship between fellow sufferers is a special one. A partnership so strong, so intimate, it's as if they are twins bonded together in a carnal need to survive.

  We started on Purple Day, March 26th[9] and I'll be co-facilitating UPLIFT[7] once more starting on April 25th. This time with Dawn of the EAC, maybe in the fall with Dr. Samson. These volunteer activities and getting back to poetry and the odd journal entry help. I'm not feeling the suicidal ideations that I had this time last year. My meds have changed, and the dose increased, which has eliminated those for now. And yet, I still have pieces of me wandering in a daze. Searching for a reality that fades in and out. Out of sync, no longer cohesive. Fragmented pictures moving in and out of focus, unglued thoughts empty. Wandering through time and space, I'm clueless about my surroundings, blind and uncomprehending. My actions are involuntary, unstoppable, not forced yet bend to the demands of mind control.

I'm bleeding, turned inside out. I'm out of strength, weak, and unconscious. Alone and unable to feel, I'm numb. The whole which is now broken and in pieces. Images of snapshots within a video in slow motion inhibited by chemicals. Influenced from an outer source, offering strength to override my weakness and pain. The searing, excruciating, and endless pain.

Unanswered questions, and the ignorance of battling illness. Another incident of ripping, a tearing apart from the essence no longer together. Chunks missing some broken and pieces floating within a bubble carried away in the wind. Untethered emotions crashing together in total destruction and turmoil. A disturbed mind fighting for the balance of thought only remains disjointed, out of kilter. Depressed and suppressed. Memories hidden, locked away from mirrors and light, kept in darkness without healing.

I don't know who I am, how I feel, if I hurt deep down inside. I'm ignorant, desensitized to my needs, and insensitive to my struggles. If I appear different, no one looks at me, and I'm left standing alone in the corner talking to myself. Why do we turn a blind eye to abuse? Allow bullying and ridicule the weak and the suffering just because? Why am I thought to be dumb, mentally incapacitated only because my brain malfunctions at times? My disability, my FND[2] with seizures, is questionable in some circles. Considered a psychological illness without a physical cause, I'm thought to be faking it and I can control it, and only looking for attention. Who cares that I also have epilepsy, uncontrolled with similar seizures? That there's no proof of which I've had. Emergency departments don't have the resources or time for a proper diagnosis, and assume you've had a 'pseudo seizure', as many still call them. Encountering constant skepticism leaves you wondering, are they right? Am I causing them? Is it my fault? I shouldn't be here. I don't belong. But I have nowhere to go.

Journal Entry, April 24, 2022

Confusion, disoriented, my vision affected. Devon and I got separated at Safeway. I tried to text and call but couldn't see the phone icons. The screen was blank. Twitching, I believe.

Journal Entry, July 1, 2022

(emailed note to myself word-for-word as typed on my phone)

Cc Ould have sworn I'd typed the entry fee or Aug 21st but after typing Aug 22nd I looked and missed a whole entry Both were on same page. Double vision plus reg vision had been fading in and out Focal impaired seizure? Or simple partial? Feeling of panic preceded sometime before followed by fogginess discoordinatoo6.

Same panic-like sensation, briefly only a second or two. Fine for a while. While typing notes, vision acting up trouble focusing, double vision worsened. Maybe a simple partial episode? Typing a section of notes, felt like I'd read it, but realized after had missed it entirely but had placed that heading above the next section. Focusing issues worsened, became disoriented, clumsily uncoordinated. Troubles eating, left side mouth worse than usual. Tingling hand like yesterday slightly stronger. Went and laid down for an hour.

Journal Entry, July 1-17, 2022

I've not been the best at documenting things. This month so far, I've experienced waves and a day and a half where I had trouble staying awake, like back in December 2014. Not the same 'flu' type feelings, but not 100%. Also, two nights ago, my right arm shot out to the side. Not so much a jerk or twitch, but a definite movement of the entire arm swinging out to the side and back.

Journal Entry, July 27, 2022

Saw Dr. Jenny today, the first appointment since June 1st. I'm three months seizure free, and the Peer-to-Peer program[8] started on March 26th. I'm co-facilitating the UPLIFT[7] session from April 25th to June 27th. My last seizure was on April 24th. I'm back to regular reflexology and massage sessions. Two sessions each, twice per month. And I got hearing aids on June 28th. Life is good right now.

Journal Entry, July 28, 2022

I had a seizure at home. Similar symptoms to the November 10, 2021, seizure at Canadian Tire or maybe Safeway. I was crawling on the floor. Received three doses of Midazolam and a Dilantin dump. My postictal period lasted for hours, and I fell off the commode in the emergency. I had to use a walker three or four times to prove I could walk before I was discharged.

Dev's observations

At about 10:30am, you call for me because a seizure is starting. You try to move to the couch futon, thingy, but don't make it. I ask you to lie down. You then kinda start crawling around the floor. Like the Canadian Tire one. You say you can't breathe and say yes when I ask if you want me to call an ambulance. They arrive around 10:50am and do their thing, give you midazolam. However it's spelled lol. They take you to Foothills around 11:10am. That is about the gist of what I recall.

Journal Entry, July 30, 2022

What is this feeling inside me? This jumbled up string of electricity humming through my nerves and frying out the ends. I don't know why or how I should be. All I know is I'm lost and lonely. I fear for my child. I fear for my family, and I feel useless, and cut off. I can't believe what they say. They say I have a mind that isn't okay. A mind that starts and stops, pausing for minutes and loses moments of time. I've lost my memories. My hands shake and tremor and I toss and turn when I sleep. If I sleep. I've shed so many tears I'm surprised I haven't shrivelled up and blown away.

Journal Entry, August 4–11, 2022

I'm having periods of light-headedness and feeling woozy my left hand tingles and 'jerks.' It's like a jolt of electricity inside, mainly on the left side of the neck down. They've occurred three or four times now. They started about a month ago.

Journal Entry, August 11, 2022

Excruciating pains on the right top of head, and the frontal lobe lasting ten to fifteen seconds. I'd put the pain level at a ten. Vivid dreams are back, those weird ones of past coworkers who'd never met, set in bizarre situations outrageous, and illogical, the details foggy and incomprehensible. Maybe I'm getting more deep sleep than REM. I've been clenching my teeth a lot. Hard. So hard I've created new grooves in my night guard.

Journal Entry, August 12, 2022

Slept well. Seven hours and forty-four minutes. Had those 'jerks' on the right-side upper body and my right thigh is sore and tight. Sharp head pains on the right-side front, mostly. Not as severe as last night and shorter.

Journal Entry, August 13, 2022

Bad head pains again, pain level down to eight. Slept well. Seven hours. My left hand was slightly tingly, as well as was the lower left lip. A touch woozy and lightheaded, anxious-type feelings in my stomach and chest. Some jerk-type actions while in bed last night, on the right side.

Journal Entry, August 19, 2022

No sharp pains on the right forehead or even the top of head over the last day or two. Spoke to Dr. Malcolm about them on Wednesday. He wasn't concerned. My prescription has changed, and he added a third eye drop to keep the pressure down. Cancelled all my appointments for today and Sunday. Not sure I'll make it into the SMU on Tuesday. I'm tired.

I've been sitting outside to get warm, but with the breeze and despite it being thirty degrees, I'm cold. Even my housecoat isn't helping.

Journal Entry, August 21, 2022

Tested positive for COVID! I can't blame Devon for infecting me. Going to the hospital every week to volunteer would increase my chances of catching it. Cancelled both the massage and reflexology appointments and resigned myself to a week of surfing from bed to couch and back again with the odd bathroom and kitchen break.

Journal Entry, September 6, 2022

I haven't slept well this week—less than six hours each night. I'm a little worried about my appointments. I see the Ophthalmologist today. Hopefully, we can do something other than prisms to correct my double vision. They're just not working and are only a temporary fix lasting less than a month or two. So frustrating. Maybe Botox will be the next step. But if the prisms and Botox don't work, at what point do we look at surgery? Or are there any other options? Botox injections would be every three months while waiting for surgery. Surgery comes with all the usual risks plus a low risk of blindness. It's possible an overcorrection could occur, but we can fix it. Surgery is a permanent fix versus the prisms.

Pains again on the right-side frontal lobe at the temple plus above and below the eyebrow. Pain level an eight or nine, very short duration of ten seconds or so. They cluster occurring up to three at a time. My nose is irritating me again. Maybe the time of year? Or the result of COVID? The right ear is plugged and sloshy. An ear infection? Who knows? Coughing still, and choking on saliva periodically, just generally worse.

Will monitor it over the next few days. Maybe I'll book an appointment with Dr. Allisen. There's been a warm, heavy, burning feeling in my stomach, like a big rock is sitting there, combined with a slight wavy uprising.

Journal Entry, September 8, 2022

Saw the shrink today. I'm doing better. The last seizure was on July 28th and the doctor in emergency feels it was an epileptic one. It was three months and three days since the previous one. The longest I've gone since 2019 or 2020. I'm volunteering in the SMU and with the EAC, co-facilitating the UPLIFT[7] program. I've been typing out all my notes and journals since 2015 and I'm amazed how far I've come since then. It's given me a new perspective on my situation and volunteering has opened my eyes to the varied and complex cases affecting people with epilepsy. My anxiety levels are down substantially, but are still there lurking in the background. Overall, I would say my mood has improved and I'm feeling more positive about life. Other health issues are slowly being dealt with. I purchased hearing aids, and I'm on the surgical wait list for my double vision. I bought myself a new bed, an adjustable bed and I'm sleeping much better. Both my son and I got COVID last month. It wasn't too bad. I survived it without having seizures, and I'm no longer scared now that I've had it. I'm going out more by myself. But unfortunately, my stomach is still bloated, and I've continued experiencing vice grip-like pressure and head pains.

Journal Entry, September 19, 2022

I was walking to my hearing appointment when a wave hit. A nauseous feeling with some rising lasting only five to fifteen seconds. I couldn't remember filling my water glass before leaving, I might have been distracted thinking about the appointment today.

Journal Entry, September 25, 2022

Had nauseous wavy feelings in the cab on the way to the SMU and then while visiting with patients. A similar feeling plus light-headedness, each lasting from one to two minutes, maybe less. More head pains on the right side today, including a slight vice grip pressure in the evening. At bedtime, a powerful wave hit after settling in bed.

Journal Entry, October 2, 2022

Didn't sleep well, less than five hours, woke feeling hungover, wavy and some nausea type anxious feelings in my gut at 9pm after showering. The back of my head is sore like I'd whacked it, and there's a funny smell like pot or something burning. Last three days, a funny metallic taste.

Journal Entry, October 5, 2022

Saw Dr. Young today. I recounted all the waves and wavy feelings I've had since the start of the year. Mentioned the nausea, pins and needles on my face and left hand and the head pains. Even included the body jerks, or jolts, as I referred to them, and the smells and funny tastes, and the anxious feelings. Dr. Young and his resident reviewed the information I provided and agreed to my request to remove the Dilantin. The weaning process will take eight months to complete. Dr. Young wants to go slow so the plan will be to drop the dose by 50mg each month. I'll start tomorrow by reducing the dose from 400mg to 350mg.

Journal Entry, October 7, 2022

With my multitude of experiences, and having both seizure types, I can offer others some hope. Hope of an altered existence that is still fulfilling. I can show that despite the three surgeries and the various meds, the severity of my seizures have lessened, albeit they're still abnormally long. I'm on fewer medications and although my cognitive functions are slightly impaired, I'm functional. I can read, write, watch tv, do crossword puzzles, and volunteer. Do I forget things? Yes. Do I have vision impairments? Yes. Balance issues? An internal compass no longer magnetized to the north. Yes. Hearing problems, sounds I don't know are there, others so overwhelming I can not bear them? Yes. But I can walk, talk, eat, sleep, write, and read. I've survived.

Journal Entry, week of October 31 to November 4, 2022

Been having the odd wave sensation. Not panicky like my anxious wavy feelings, more like the old waves, but not quite as strong. Maybe related to the Dilantin weaning? Who knows? My sleep is disrupted somewhat with the reduced dosage. Was trying not to take the Melatonin but started taking 5mg per night again. Some tingling in the hand and a couple of feelings of light-headedness. Related to the waves? Sleep changes? Been doing well with the reduced dose and, I've exceeded the three-month seizure free mark! As of November 4th, today, it's been three months and six days?! Better than last time. Hopefully, now that UPLIFT[7] has finished for the year, my SMU visits, and increase in exercise and better eating habits, will get me to four or five months of seizure freedom.

The longer I can go without either type, will improve the depression and anxiety.

Journal Entry, November 5, 2022

Been so tired lately. Other than the occasional night, I've slept well, an average of seven hours. Dev's been the same despite our increased walks. He figures it's a fallout from COVID. Probably, but may also be due in part to my Dilantin weaning. My dose is down only 50mg but maybe combined with the side effects of COVID my sleep has suffered. I reached the three-month mark again. Three months and seven days, eight if nothing today. UPLIFT[7] finished up on Thursday, but I still have my visits to the SMU.

It's taken longer than I'd hoped, but maybe I've regained some control over my life. I hope so, cause let's face it, I'm not having any more surgeries, no more stays in the SMU. There's nothing they can do for me now besides tweaking meds and some therapy now and again. Which is a good thing. Again, not what I'd hope for. Not what my original prognosis and surgical outcome had projected. But, hey. It's me. The medical super freak, not really, but it sounds good, lol. I'm the enigma, the mystery, the complex case showing signs of a progressive situation for an illness which isn't. *Sigh*. I guess I don't like 'easy'. I appear to enjoy being that 'difficult' patient who won't fit into the stereotypical box I should belong in. Oh well. Such is life. It is what it is. Everything happens for a reason and a reason to when things will happen and to whom they happen to. So many platitudes I've told myself over the years. Excuses? Maybe. Feeling sorry for myself? Yes and no. Self blame? Depression? Probably, knowing myself as I do. So much is out of my control no matter what I try, what I do or don't. And I dislike it! Anyway, no point dwelling over what was. Can't change it. A part of my brain is gone, the rest functioning at a pace slower than before. Permanently injured, no chance of recovering to presurgical norms, forever altered, damaged, not the same. My left side will continue to have the deficits caused by the last surgery, losing the sensation and dexterity it once had. Acceptance of this is crucial to allow progress, to move forward compensating for what was and will not be again. We can't fix some things. Some things remain broken, no matter how hard we try to repair them.

Wow! I guess I needed this. A brain dump. An emotional confession from mind to page. It's amazing how much lighter I feel afterwards. A weight is lifted, allowing me to sit up, and stand straighter.

Journal Entry, November 8, 2022

I am so glad to be involved in the Peer-to-Peer Program[8], to aid in growing the epilepsy community and be a support to others through the UPLIFT[7] program. It is a wonderful feeling to be needed, appreciated, and among others who understand what I'm going through, and have access to support for my mental health, to complete my care offering.

Meeting patients of all ages, genders, and races while visiting the seizure unit is an enlightening experience. So often people with epilepsy do not get the opportunity to meet others with a similar diagnosis. So focused on our own experiences and how to manage them, we're not often exposed to other experiences and seizure types.

Even with all of the reading I've done, I learn something new after each visit to the seizure unit. Talking to patients with the same seizure types as myself, offers insight into how varied the seizures can be. When I was diagnosed, I had both focal aware seizures and focal impaired. My focal impaired events were longer than normal, occurring every two to four months. Others I've met with the same seizure types, may not experience them the way I do.

I recall on more than one occasion encountering those whose focal impaired seizures were much shorter than mine but would occur in clusters, i.e. the frequency between seizures were shorter, some occurring multiple times in a day. The effects of their episodes were far more disabling than any of mine, and the only hope for seizure control was either a new combination of medications or surgery. Having tried all the meds available for focal seizures plus the three temporal lobe surgeries, I could share my experiences offering comfort and an understanding of the trials and errors of refractory (drug-resistant) epilepsy.

My moods have improved with the new antidepressant. My seizure activity is slowing, only three visits to the emergency this year. I'm now weaning off the Dilantin, Yay! Leaving me with just the Lamotrigine to manage the epileptic seizures. The functional seizures are under control for the most part with the addition of the Peer-to-Peer[8] visits to the SMU and my participation in UPLIFT[7].

2022 has been the best year so far, health-wise, since we moved here three years ago. My overall health is improving, Dev has made some friends and is doing well in school. Life is good.

Journal Entry, November 17, 2022

'The call'. I don't recall ever returning for a repeat mammogram before, let alone needing an ultrasound, as well. When I went last week, I mentioned a 'lump' under the right breast, which I felt was a zit refusing to pop. Not sure what showed up, but they want to take another look and perform an ultrasound. I've been trying hard not to overreact. Not to execute the usual knee jerk reaction of doom and gloom. I can't go down that road of thinking I'm dying, that I have cancer, that it will snuff my life out before it should. Just as things are improving and for the first time I'll be on one anti-seizure medication once I've finished the Dilantin weaning.

I have eight days to go to reach the four-month seizure free mark. Four months of no ambulance rides, waking up in emergency hours later, doped up and weak. I feel better, emotionally, feel like doing things again. The gym, walks, cooking, organizing, amongst other things.

Journal Entry, November 18, 2022

I'm trying to convince myself the recall appointment is nothing. It's just a precaution, or a zit, the scar tissue from the reduction, or from gaining weight. I've gained 5kg, the highest gain in a long time. It'll be fine. I'm not going anywhere yet.

Journal Entry, November 23, 2022

Life amazes me. Since my epilepsy and FND[2] diagnoses, my view of the world has altered dramatically, as it would for anyone with a chronic illness. The stigma attached to epilepsy and mental illnesses still exists today. Not much has really changed since the early days. Society still assumes grand mal seizures are what all people with epilepsy have when, in fact, there are over forty different types, many of which can occur without the casual observer even knowing.

I never was a big supporter of meditation until my dual diagnoses. The need to relax, breathe, and calm myself was not part of my thought processes. I would stifle the feelings, ignore the emotions, and carry on accepting these instances as normal. Everyone experienced them. I wasn't any different, just needed to be stronger. But I was wrong. (At least in my situation I was). Today, I manage my stress using the skills I've learned. I breathe through my fears, control my anxieties and depression by staying present, being in the moment. Not forecasting a future I have no control over and a past that was, frankly, in the past. I can't change those moments in time, cannot recapture them. No mulligans, no re-dos. No, 'if I knew then what I know now' wishes. It's taken a while. It's a process. An ongoing trial and error, a practice, practice, and more practice scenario. And it helps. I know this by experiencing it. I know this because I see it in others. Since August 2021, I've volunteered my time on the neurological floor, visiting patients admitted for a plethora of reasons. Brain surgeries, onset of dementia, Alzheimer's and many other conditions. Seen loneliness and depression and empathized with their pain and anxieties. I could relate on so many levels.

Journal Entry, November 26, 2022

It's been a rough week filled with a mammogram and an eye appointment, but no seizures. My left hand has been tingly and numb. I've felt lightheaded, wavy and with moments of nausea. My sleep has been ok, not the best but also not my worst. Overall, I'm not doing too bad, I guess and despite the stress of my other health issues, my seizure activity has dropped this year.

Journal Entry, November 29, 2022

I made it! Four months without a seizure! Four months of no ambulances, no drugs pumped into my system, causing a deep drowsiness akin to a coma lasting for hours. Four months of no seizures despite contracting COVID. Am I free of my seizures? What happens next month when my Dilantin dose drops another 50mg? I'm worried the seizures will increase once the Dilantin weaning is finished. Despite the mental fog that's lifting, anxiety levels rise as each month approaches. And with each drop so too does the hours of sleep I get each night, and the combination of both lowers my seizure threshold.

I know I shouldn't think about it, that I can't control my future, and I shouldn't concern myself over something that may not happen. I can't stress over the unknown. But it's hard not to. Hard not to look ahead and ensure I'm not overloading the days and overwhelming myself with back-to-back activities. Keep from wearing myself down, lowering my defences and reducing my seizure threshold. It's difficult to focus on the moment, the day, the immediate space in time. To constantly remind myself to breathe, scan my body in search of pressure points of tension. Using all the skills I've learned from UPLIFT[7] and the talk therapy with Drs. Harper and Jenny, plus the antidepressants prescribed by Dr. McKay.

Although I hadn't any 'big' seizures, I have experienced moments of waves, nausea-type sensations, the odd twitch of the mouth on the left, tingly hand and arm, lightheaded and moments of dizziness, and drowsy. But nothing evolved past those brief sensations, no full-blown event, and if my functional seizures are truly under control, then these brief moments are epileptic in nature, and I could tolerate them. I knew the last surgery wouldn't 'cure' me, and I would continue having seizures, but if the last surgery corralled the worst of them, I could handle these less disruptive ones. I must learn to accept my life as it is and live my remaining years to the best of my abilities.

Journal Entry, December 1, 2022

Wow. The last days of 2022 are upon us. Three hundred and thirty some days came and went, brief sections of a whole gobbled up and spat out. It's been a year. Better than the last two, but not without its own peaks and valleys, the good, bad, ugly and beautiful.

Journal Entry, December 3, 2022

Still no seizures, at least not the ones that send me to the emergency. I'm hoping the seizures are under wraps. Three years since the official diagnosis, over two years of therapy, oodles of UPLIFT[7] sessions, meditations, exercise, poetry, writing my memoir, journaling, a new antidepressant, volunteering, and over four months without an ambulance ride.

But the last two weeks I've been fighting it. I can feel it. The tingling hand and vibrating lip, and the mini risings that go nowhere, thank God. Nausea-type sensations, feeling lightheaded and dazed. Talking myself down, breathing, focusing on my whole body, not just the parts, keeping busy distracting myself, shifting my thoughts elsewhere.

It's been a struggle and today has been the worse, but I've calmed my fears and controlled my body. Baking, music, organizing, cleaning, bingeing on Disney+, audiobooks and crosswords, all to keep sane. So far, it's working.

Journal Entry, December 6, 2022

I'm struggling to keep the lid on, forcing the rising storm back down. My hand tingles, the pinkie finger numb, as are the next two. Deadened nerves short circuiting vainly struggling to jump start the motor within, to generate power to the tips and restore the sensation.

Twelve more days and it'll be five months since my last seizure. My last ambulance ride, emergency visit, and a body flooded with drugs. Another seventeen days and it'll be eleven years since my first seizure. December 23, 2011. That was the start of everything. The start of a molecular change that altered my inner being. The onset of memory loss, personality changes, and a journey down a path of fear, loneliness, depression, and pain. A life so different from what I imagined. A new beginning that spiralled out of control, spinning round and round. An existence of instability and life-changing decisions. December sucks!

Journal Entry, December 10, 2022

I'm not sleeping well again. Going to bed too late and waking early. I guess it's the stress of finishing the Xmas baking, planning the distribution, and failed Nanaimo bars. And, being December, my month of unhappiness and grief. My ex's death one week before Christmas 2006, the decision to leave Daniel, and, of course, that first seizure on December 23, 2011.

It's been eighteen years of hell. It's no wonder I'm tired, fed up, frustrated and angry. It's been an uphill battle, but there is a silver lining, a flicker of light through a pinhole. I'm just over four months since the last seizure. My Dilantin dose is reducing. I can see the top of the mountain. My life will plateau and my view of the future, while still challenging, will become easier.

I've been experiencing wavelike sensations. Lightheaded, a slight rising, tired, brief moments of sleep, like blanking out. A constant buzz of nerves in my left hand, memory blips, and a forgotten batch of cookies in the oven. Forgetting where I put my phone, glasses, water glass, and coffee mug. Words are there, but just out of reach. Mouth vibrating like a twitch about to start.

Journal Entry, December 16, 2022

Had a couple moments of wave type sensations and felt lightheaded last two days. No twitching. Just a cotton batten feeling numbing my perception of things. Fully aware as in knowing the tv is on, can hear it, see the images moving but from a distance. My right eye and lower lip were twitching but the sensation in my hand, even my left ear and side of face, was muted. No twitching and the tingling almost non-existent. The double vision seems worse even after the last Botox injection. Doesn't matter if I use the temporary prism or go without glasses or if I use my older ones with no prism.

Journal Entry, December 23, 2022

My book *Battles of The Mind* is just about ready to publish on KDP.

I've created the cover, re-read the entire book, adjusting here and there. I've changed the names of hospitals in BC but kept Foothills. I feel I'm safe in doing so since I've sung the praises of the services and staff. I'll also include a disclaimer that the events portrayed are from my recollection, from a memory dulled by medication, high anxiety and depression. The details within its pages pieced together from journal entries, test results, and summaries of procedures and events taken place as stated in doctor reports and letters. I can't be faulted for any omissions, errors, exaggerations by a mind altered by the physical and emotional. With Devon's help, I should be able to upload this book today or tomorrow. I'd really like to get it off my plate, move forward. Focus on a poetry book, my blog, and improving my health.

Journal Entry, December 31, 2022

No 'big' seizures, thank God. I've finally reached five months without one, the last being July 28th. The eye twitching seems to have gone; the tingling has settled down. There were a few occasions when a wave began rushing over me, then suddenly stopped. Anxiety? I don't know. It's happened during the day and just after crawling into bed. Sporadic. If I were to guess, an average of one to two times per week.

I ended the year weaning down to 300mg of Dilantin, a drop of 100mg. Considering the stress of the mammogram, my vision issues, and the probability of two eye surgeries in 2023, I've done well. In January the Dilantin will drop another 50mg reducing it to 250mg.

I've come a long way since 2015 dealing with a crap tonne of drama and turmoil. And being me, it couldn't be just the epilepsy, it had to include FND[2], glaucoma, double vision, ear, and throat issues, a dysfunctional left hand, periodic gallbladder attacks, and now a lump on my right breast.

There's been many battles won and advancements made, which have improved my overall mental health. But not one to place much faith on a new year, learned the hard way what happens when I do, I'll just trust that 2023 will continue this new path I'm on and carry me closer to the light at the end of the tunnel.

2022—A Year of Hope and Moving Ahead

Another day, another week, a new month, the last month. Where in the heck did the year go?

I'm starting to believe the adage that time slips away faster as you get older. I recall as a child, wishing the days away to reach a long awaited day, a special occasion, only to have the hours and minutes tick by at the rate of a snail on ice. Then, as you got older, those special times become fewer and farther between. So bogged down in the responsibilities of the day-to-day grind, the days slip by unnoticed. The days blur, weeks meld into each other, one constant trail with no end. As the ticker tape of daily life spins by, those hours and minutes add up and before you know it, a month has gone by. Then another. And another. And soon all twelve have come and gone and a new year looms ahead.

It's hard to believe we've been here in Calgary for *three* years now. A new home, of old familiar places and faces mixed in with fresh places and spaces. A pandemic. Losing family and a friend. A family closer in distance yet still far apart compounding that sense of isolation.

2022 has been a year of promise, and new hope, with the slow resumption of a normality we all lost. And yet, for many, it's been a year of progress, new beginnings, the start of new travels exciting and scary. For me, 2022 was a continuation of the same old trials. A smaller sized version of a roller coaster, with fewer bumps and potholes to navigate. This year had fewer seizures, ambulances, and hospital visits, and more pros versus cons. I've ticked several boxes on my to do list of ailments. Hearing aids, eye drops and Botox injections have cleared up my distorted view of the world around me allowing the beauty of sight and sound to enter within.

What's in store for 2023? Don't know. I gave up making new year's resolutions years ago, refusing to create a no-win situation by setting the bar so high I'd always trip and fall. Living with epilepsy and FND[2] with seizures, being depressed, anxious, and having suicidal ideations, my goal is to focus on the here and now, not dwell on the past or pining for a future I couldn't control. Being mindful of the now, aware of this moment in time, and how it affects me. Managing what I can, and how I think and feel, realizing what must be, what will be, and what I must leave alone.

2023 will have its challenges, I know, but I'm a new person, a different being, stronger and wiser than before. I have the tools to manage what life can hold, the frustrations, anxieties, and emotional upheavals, and I will survive.

CHAPTER TEN

2023—New Possibilities

Of two minds and two shades, one of lightness, the other dark. Of open fields and black caves, a positive, a negative, and somewhere in between. As the sunlight shines, my spirit glows, a sprinkle here a sprinkle there as she goes. When the power goes dark and the light is gone, she hides staying safe til the light of dawn.

Like a coin with two sides, an in and an out the ups and downs. Opposites attract, so the story goes, ebbing and flowing as the ocean's tides. The inner self versus the outer shell plus the private side, I am here doing well. The innie and the outie of who I am.

Two minds the same, but not one body or one soul is what I've got. A positive, a negative, and somewhere in between. Living within a shadow, rarely appearing in daylight. Sometimes hollow, sometimes only a spark of lightness or dark; see through or not.

I live on both planes, on the positive and the negative and somewhere in between.

Journal Entry, January 1, 2023

The first of a new year, the beginning of what's coming. A jumpstart to fresh adventures, a carryover from what came before, on the brink and ready to explore. Plotting an alternative course carving out a plan for the months to come sculpting the framework from start to finish only to come full circle and begin again.

Journal Entry, January 6, 2023

A little weird. I felt pulses inside my limbs like a vibration without the external movement, but more subtle than my mouth and nothing like the pins and needles in my left hand. Anxiety related? No, more of a mild current of electricity for lack of a better example. Periodic and only noticeable while sitting. Like a floor moving from the trembling of a heavy truck or train rumbling by. Started up within the last month or so. No wave type sensations or light-headedness nor nausea.

Journal Entry, January 24, 2023

(as written in the hospital)

Seixure yesterday still on er today. They feel it was epilepti I'm nolso sure

Seizure yesterday at Foothills wa just dropped off when confusion and vision issues began.couldnr see. Screen to see if on to WiFi and AHS app progressed to bumping into things, weaving unsure of where I was going. Eventually asked for help and that's all I remember. We 0 o 24 no no No no no

Journal Entry, January 27, 2023

Here we are again worrying if another seizure will follow and uncertain which type it was. Eighteen minutes, the doctor said, long for an average epileptic one but short for a functional seizure, but then, as Dr. Young told the ER doctor, it's hard to tell with me. It was the longest I've gone without a seizure since 2015. Four days short of six months! Not bad considering my Dilantin dose has reduced since October. It could be worse.

It is funny how it happened at Foothills on my way to volunteer. Better than in the cab. It hit fast, and if I recall, a rising anxious, panicky feeling preceded it. I couldn't see the screen on my phone, stumbled along the corridor, bumped into something, called for help, then nothing. They loaded me up with Ativan and Dilantin, quite a bit from what I gather. I came to in the emergency, unaware of it all. There was some concern I had pneumonia, but they cleared me. I was so out of it they put a catheter in. It wasn't until the wee hours of yesterday morning before I could use a walker, and I'm still a bit wobbly today.

Dev must go to the Southern Alberta Institute of Technology (SAIT) today for classes. I'm nervous, as is he, to be home alone, but it'll be ok. I've got lots I can do to distract myself. Read, write, watch *The Practice*, laundry, prep for mini quiches, nap, listen to music. I'll get through it like I've always done. It'll be fine. I'll drink some chamomile tea to help calm me.

I hate I can't tell the difference between the seizures. It's frustrating and scary! I can only imagine what Dev goes through each time. Such a weight to carry so early in his adult years. It's hard enough on those much older, even those with medical experience. I'm not sure I could handle it as well as he has. Such a trooper. I'm certainly blessed.

Feeling anxious this morning. My hand is buzzing away, and I feel like throwing up. My stomach is in knots. Started drinking chamomile tea with peppermint again, hoping it'll calm me. Dev leaves for school in an hour, won't be back till after four. I've got to keep it together until then.

Journal Entry, January 28, 2023

Four days... Four days, what's a mere four days? Two times forty-eight hours, four times one; eleven thousand five hundred and twenty seconds. Wednesday, the fourth day of the week, or Thursday, depending on where you start. Four days; 1/7 of a month, give or take, a teardrop in the big scheme of things.

Four days isn't a lot of time unless counting down the days, aiming for a goal, or dreading a future event. It's such a small number yet made the difference between six months seizure free and not. Four days short I was, a tiny amount of space in the vastness of everything. Five months and twenty-seven days, four days short of my longest stint without rescue drugs, ambulance rides, and a trip to the emergency. Maybe next time.

Journal Entry, January 31, 2023

Anxious about volunteering in the SMU today. Must focus on my breathing and staying in the moment. Had a good sleep which will help. Lisa called back from Dr. Young's office. I'm to stay at 250mg of Dilantin for now unless he wants to change it. He wasn't in. She spoke to another neurologist and will forward the revised prescription to Rexall. I feel better about this. As my pharmacist said, I may just have to remain on the Dilantin to keep the seizures somewhat under control. Oh well. C'est la vie.

Journal Entry, February 1, 2023

I need to write more to remove the pent-up feelings from inside my head to paper. I'm suppressing them again, or at least I think I have. Distracting myself with Disney+ and publishing my book, I haven't been exercising, plus I'm snacking a lot and not sleeping. No wonder the seizure happened.

It's so hard to be motivated. I depend upon Dev's resolve so much that mine has disappeared. Not that I really had any. My eating habits went to shit after we moved. From the depression and anxiety, I guess. And maybe a loss of focus. Dev's grown up. He's going to school, his days occupied with studying, classes, homework, and hanging with friends. It's hard without that circle of friends to 'hang' with. Yes, I have the weekly visits to the SMU and UPLIFT,[7] when it's running, but there's still enormous gaps of time to fill. Hollow spaces that need some other form of activity besides watching tv and reading. I need movement to get the blood pumping to prove I'm still alive, not just a rotting shell in the corner.

Maybe I should get out, visit the writing centre, and socialize, write, read. Even just once a week for a few hours on Thursdays or Fridays and still do the Poetry Cafe on Sundays. It's worth thinking about. Getting out and about interacting with others with similar interests and defer to for advice.

Journal Entry, February 2, 2023

My book is done and up on Amazon, the e-book on January 7th and the paperback four days ago. Seven years it took to write with no clue of what I was doing. Thousands of dollars spent on workshops, writing programs, membership fees to associations and writing clubs. Hours hunched over my laptop spilling my guts out on a blank screen, not caring of grammar rules and story structure. Unfamiliar with submission protocols, where to look for agents and publishers. What about editing, a book cover, do I pay them to publish? Can I trust them not to steal my work? Who can I ask for help? This is so confusing, frustrating, and overwhelming to a newbie like me. Even the thought of doing it myself was scary. What if I do it wrong? How much will it cost me? Can my damaged brain handle it?

In the end, self publishing was the best option, and I couldn't have done it without Dev's help. I would have gotten so frustrated trying to format the cover and figure it all out. I'd have given up that's for sure. It's just nice to hold an actual book in my hands and say I wrote it. Now, it's a matter of marketing it.

Journal Entry, March 19, 2023

Feeling a bit off, not anxious like anything bad is happening. Hard to put it into words. On the contrary, things are going well. My book has a few excellent reviews. I met retired NHL goalie Kelly Hrudey, got Dr. Young out to The Purple Day by Night[10] event, and started recording my audio book. I joined the new International Bureau for Epilepsy Community Council. No surgical procedures are necessary for my glaucoma right now. Oh, and was invited to join a new patient advisory group with AHS Foothills Neurosurgery.

Life's been good so far in 2023. So why the tingling in my hand and mouth? Why am I still anxious about going out alone or when Dev goes to school? And why can't I resume my workouts? I've got UPLIFT[7], my SMU visits which help me as much as I help others. Yes, I've got double vision, a constant frustration, and I worry about the lump under my breast, but everything else has calmed down or are dealt with. My sleep is consistent. The hours may not always be there, but the quality is good. I'm better at saying 'no' and reducing my weekly activities and therefore my stress. Do I have lots of friends? No. But I have more support than I did. Kenneth, the EAC, Drs. Jenny, Samson, and my son. But I miss mom. She was my daily connection to the outside world. And I miss mom's old neighbour Myra and her updates on the condo building and all the changes in the area. But that's life. Things change constantly. Nothing sits still and stagnates. At least living things don't. There's a pulse, a heartbeat, the rise and fall of breathing in fresh air and expelling the stale.

I moved to Calgary to start a new life knowing I was in a safe place, a space where I'm cared for by those who understand my conditions. The knowledge and expertise are here to guide me, to help me find the calm serenity I crave. Moving to a city where the 'old me' didn't exist, where no one 'mourned' the loss of the person they once knew and loved. In Calgary, I'm just me. A stranger with all the flaws and cracks I currently own. That 'old self' hidden from view, there, but not forgotten, just not the same. I'm a hybrid, a mix of before and now, a piece of this, a part of that, and a dash of those, all jumbled up and scrambled together, projecting a new image so very different yet similar. Dents and scars cover my outer shell, while the inner core has become hard, toughened against the inner workings of an explosive mind and disturbed persona. An aura of self preservation encircles my form, there to protect, to keep out the turbulence that erodes my sanity, removing the sanctuary I created for myself.

"No, I can't" isn't a refusal to try, but the need to reduce mayhem and stress. "I won't". Is a promise to myself I won't jeopardize my sanity to appease another. "I shouldn't". A reminder of my limitations and foolishly thinking I can ignore them and carry on as I did before. "I wouldn't". The acceptance and acknowledgement of the strengths and weaknesses I live with and vowing to listen and hear what my body says and do what is right for me. It takes courage to accept who you are and who you've become. It's difficult to take a path you've never considered; never thought you'd travel. Where we started, where we've been, and how we got here almost never represent the vision we expected. Too often outside forces inhibit the process, steering us in another direction with different views, different pitfalls, resulting in an outcome you'd never expected. It's what you do with it and how you react to your new surroundings that matter. Sometimes it is the journey that molds you, but not always. Sometimes, it's your reactions to the unexpected, the surreal, that grants you the wisdom and strength to move onto the next adventure.

Remember, live for the moment. Relinquish that which you can not control. Focus on today, not yesterday, or tomorrow. Have faith in yourself and all those around you. Despite all your challenges, the feelings of isolation, depression, and anxiety, remember this: you're not alone.

Journal Entry, April 30, 2023

I feel lost, a solitary shape with no outline, a flimsy cloud of gas people pass through, oblivious of my presence. Unimportant, an after thought, depressing, forgetful, boring because of my limitations. A misunderstood neurological disorder often thought of as fake. Another that should have magically disappeared with drugs and surgery. I'm a hermit behind closed doors, within my impenetrable fortress of high walls to hide behind. I did not ask for this, wanted no part of two seizure disorders which tore me apart, creating a person I'd never recognize. A calendar filled with doctor appointments and tests, no longer a social butterfly attending concerts and sporting events, going to movies and parties. All things of the past. Self-preservation is the number one priority vs. living, really living, a stagnant flat line of unstimulating life, an existence of quiet. All energy focused on maintaining the status quo, being alone, reducing stress, self healing mindfulness, aware of the now not then or when. A constant battle of the mind, a war raging in the cortex of my being, fighting against physical sensations and emotions, each struggling to gain the upper hand. Who'd have known such things live within a spirit once outgoing and carefree? A new world of challenges, obstacles to overcome alone. I'm tired, weary, frustrated, and angry. Angered by the erosion of what I'd been, how my life, although not perfect, seemed fuller and happier. No hurdle blocked my path indefinitely, I had alternatives at my disposal to fight my struggles and rise above.

Journal Entry, May 9, 2023

I'm feeling weird, lost in a way, juggling so many balls I'm waiting for that one to drop. Had those vibrations in my mouth. My left hand surging on and off, feeling numb and sensitive at the same time, as if the nerves were just under the first layer of skin. Wavy anxious type sensations, more wave than anxiety, have resurfaced plus the head pains. Weather related? Menopause? Maybe? Oh, and those prickly sensations on my shin are back, the right more than left. Seizure related? Who knows? If so, not much can be done. Part of me feels 'cast aside' since my FND[2] diagnosis. Like it's all I have. No epileptic seizures, only those caused by my emotions and stress levels, the fallout from the last eight years. Yeah, the epilepsy is still there but is now a passenger not sitting behind the wheel. Am I depressed? No, I don't think so. Am I hiding behind those old stone walls? Maybe. My life has a new direction, a different focus than before. Volunteering. The International Bureau for Epilepsy (IBE), Epilepsy Association of Calgary (EAC), and Seizure Monitoring Unit (SMU) all worthwhile ventures offering support, understanding, education, and awareness fulfilling my new purpose in life. The void I needed to fill since my epilepsy diagnosis. Even more so since they confirmed my FND[2]. My mental state, already screwed up, scrambled even more by illness and death these last three years thanks to COVID. The timing of new support programs at the EAC couldn't have been better. I'm thankful from an epilepsy point of view, but those same resources are lacking, almost nonexistent for those with both epilepsy and FND[2] with seizures. The medical system is to blame for that. Not enough funding for mental health programs. Basic CBT and mindfulness techniques would address so many issues surrounding depression, anxiety, stress, and trauma. You'd think governments would see this, address it, acknowledge it, and take measures to implement support networks. But I must admit, only after my own experiences with severe depression, suicidal ideations, and anxiety levels off the chart did I understand the failings of the mental health system.

Journal Entry, June 9, 2023

Is it wrong to cocoon myself from the future and restrict the possibilities of negative results? Is it bad to feel anxious about what I can't control and therefore reduce my exposure to pain and suffering? That I know what my limitations are and I'm forced to live by them. To do what's right for me and the hell with what others may think?

Anxiety, depression, loneliness, sadness, and pain all negative emotions arising from life interrupted. A reaction to an action, all honest expressions of my inner turmoil, a rippling effect of a smooth surface disturbed by sensations no longer contained, and the rebounding effect of a scream echoing over the airwaves. To divert from the negative to positive takes practice, strength, and purpose. But is it always necessary? Must I never allow myself to acknowledge the darkness? Must I only recognize the light and refuse to look backwards? Are those deep shadows of black always evil? Could they fade and move into the background as I move forward? And yet to exist only in one or the other isn't plausible, is irrational, and defies the realm of an emotional experience. Without feelings, I am nothing. To ignore them doesn't deter them. There's nowhere for them to go but out. Whether expressed verbally or physically, they'll have their say. They'll have their day in the spotlight, regardless of what I want or wish. FND[2] with seizures is just one mechanism of such an expression. A means of escape from my troubled mind. A way to be heard without the restrictions, bindings and chains weighing them down. No longer hidden. And yet it is possible to stem the flow and reduce the surge. Just by experiencing the emotion when it occurs and letting it wash over me can limit its impact, reducing the tide before it swells, growing larger and larger as it moves in.

Journal Entry, June 12, 2023

Another seizure on Saturday. Epileptic? Maybe. No shaking. Just sitting in the computer chair. Leaning to the left, body somewhat rigid, staring off into space, nonresponsive, verbally, and physically. Ativan seemed to help, then stopped. 911 and the inevitable trip to Foothills. Don't recall arriving in the emergency bay, only awakened as they wheeled me into the emergency. Blood tests were normal, some questions about the blood gasses and ECG if I read the results right. But obviously nothing untoward since they discharged me. Had some waves, tingly mouth, prickly sensations leading up to it. Since January's event, I'd been working on the audiobook, added the IBE Community Council to my list of activities, and trying to focus on writing. My eating and exercise habits are up and down as well as my sleep.

Journal Entry, June 23, 2023

I've lost my purpose, unsure of where I'm heading, if anywhere. My book is complete, nothing more to do. Not doing a hardcover, they don't sell. No UPLIFT[7] until the fall. I still have the weekly visits to the SMU, but other than an appointment or two, I've nothing for the summer. No plans, to-do lists, and no trips. But then, where would I go? I'm tired and maybe depressed. My only social life is at Foothills. SMU visits and check-ins with Kenneth, UPLIFT[7] sessions and nothing else. I want to go to the writing centre but feel so restricted on time. Booking a return trip with Calgary Transit Access will spoil the natural flow of writing and yet a cab costs too much. I'm stuck in a rut and the sides are crumbling, burying me under dirt and rocks. I feel useless and pull strength from Dev just to keep moving when all I want is to hide away and let someone else take care of things. Plan the meals, do the cooking, dust, and vacuum, and clean my space, letting me just be. The thought of a retirement home has become quite appealing. Ready-made activities, gatherings over meals and just because. The option to be alone or socialize without the cares of every day would be nice. I'm tired and bored.

Journal Entry, July 1, 2023

Am I depressed? Beginning the downward spiral into my darkened hole? I don't know. Maybe? Since I published *Battles of The Mind*, I don't know what to do with myself. And with UPLIFT[7] done for the summer, it's only added to the loss of purpose. It could be I'm feeling lost, unsure of where to go or if there's somewhere I want to go to? I've worked on my memoir for seven years, on and off. I've learned a lot about writing a book, the editing, and publishing, tapping into emotions buried deep below the surface. Between that and the seizures, moving, COVID, and losing mom, I've focused on the day to day. I struggled, forged on, stumbled, and fell, yet found the strength to get up and carry on. But now. Now I've arrived at my destination. The seizures have settled from the turbulent storms they had been. Not dispersed completely, but no longer a weekly or monthly occurrence.

I have my volunteer work, but not much else. Haven't seen my family and my only 'friends' are Kenneth and the staff at Foothills and Angie our lovely leasing agent for our building. I'm partly to blame, restricting my activities both financially and medically.

Maybe other authors go through this when the book is done, and the next is unclear, and they mourn the loss like an empty nester whose children have left home. There's a silence now, like a conversation that has abruptly ended, or the train of thought derailed. Am I depressed? Not sure. Am I sad? Probably. Am I lonely? Maybe. I'm lost in a sea of unknowns with no life preservers or flotation devices to keep me afloat. I'm a mere speck of a smudge on an otherwise flawless picture. An insignificant grain of sand among a landscape stretching for miles. A solitary figure isolated and alone, moving silently through shadows undetected and devoid of colour, its lights dimmed. I have no purpose other than being. My direction only stagnant and stale, mourning the loss of what was and unsure whether to go or just stand still.

Journal Entry, July 11, 2023

I don't know what's wrong with me today. I'm so tired, lost in a fog, unsure of what to do. Sad, defeated almost. I'm weepy and feel like crying until my eyes dry up. I haven't slept well, and this stupid stampede hasn't helped. The booming bass from that tent is so annoying and Coco waking me early doesn't help. My mood is down. I don't want to do anything, go anywhere, or talk to anyone. Am I burnt out? Has the previous six months finally caught up with me? A delayed reaction to all the stress and pressure I've placed on myself. Probably. The rent is going up, Coco's health costs are rising, I need glasses, and last year's breast cancer scare which was only a cyst has now been replaced with a possible heart condition. I need a break. I need time to think and just do nothing.

Journal Entry, September 8, 2023

My twenty-nine-year-old baby. His first time in the hospital since birth. His first surgery. My irrational mind creating unrealistic scenarios adding to my stress, disturbing my sleep. It's been difficult keeping the cap screwed on to avoid triggering a seizure. It still is, although he came through the surgery and is back at home doing well. Must be the aftereffects of the last month or two. The gradual escalation of stress and the battle to keep sane and not dive off the deep end.

On a positive note, I got through the night on my own while Dev was in the hospital. A major achievement.

Journal Entry September 26, 2023

I had a seizure last Monday. Was at the hospital on my way to the SMU to volunteer. It's now the third time I've had a seizure at Foothills during my scheduled visit.

The wavy sensations began in the lobby and increased as I stepped into the elevator. I pressed eleven on the touchscreen and…the rest is foggy. For all I know, I stood on that elevator going up and down while others came and went. For how long I don't know.

I recall pressing eleven once more, hearing a voice say, "We're going down." The next thing I remember is the doors opening and stumbling out, "I'm having a seizure" were the last words I heard. A vague recollection of shuffling on my butt, a voice questioning the Psychogenic non-epileptic seizures (PNES[1]) written on the tattoo on my arm. Then nothing. Just an empty, dark space. It could have been later that day or the next when I awakened to find myself in a hospital bed. Drugged up and confused, I still knew I was safe. As my consciousness surfaced, I knew it was an epileptic seizure, not a functional one.

Although Dr. Young says it's difficult to tell with me, this time, I was sure. The sudden confusion, loss of awareness, no twitching that I knew confirming I was right.

Stress triggers both my epileptic and functional seizures, however, lack of sleep usually signals an epileptic seizure, not the FND² so much. I'm no doctor, but even they can't tell unless I'm in the SMU with my head covered in electrodes and on video.

There isn't time or the resources in emergency to perform EEGs and the doctors and nurses not sufficiently trained to detect which is which. Regardless of the seizure type, my epileptic ones have always been exceptionally long. I've had tonic-clonic seizures, focal aware and focal unaware, and now functional seizures. No one can be sure of which I've just experienced, including myself. You'd think after eight years and countless seizures, I'd be an expert and know without a doubt which type I had. You'd think I could tell them apart. Unfortunately, it's not that simple. Whether epileptic or not, they're all just seizures to me. Some are more debilitating than others. Recovering from the crippling effects, taking hours, sometimes days. The emotional stress leading up to it and the depression and guilt that follow. Overwhelmed by anxiety and the fear of another occurring mingled with the disappointment of not attaining that magical milestone of six months of seizure freedom.

November 15, 2023, Dr. Young phone appointment

Was to see Dr. Young but I was sick. Turned out to be COVID. We conducted my appointment over the phone. My Lamotrigine levels are low, reducing their efficacy to stop seizures, but there aren't any other medications we can switch to. I've tried them all. Our plan is to increase the Lamotrigine from 200mg twice daily to 225mg twice daily. After one week at the higher dose, I'm to get blood levels checked for both Dilantin and Lamotrigine. My next follow up will be in about six to eight months.

December 13, 2023, Seizure

In bedroom on laptop when a massive wave hit. Sat for some time staring, unable to speak or move but aware of surroundings. Breathing became difficult, laboured like heavy breathing. Devon came in and tried to get me on the floor. Said I was moving around in circles on the computer chair. I slipped off the chair; the seat hitting me in the head as it swung around. He said I kept saying I couldn't breathe, asked if I wanted an Ativan and I said yes. At some point I became unresponsive, and then shortly after a tonic-clonic seizure. That was when he called 911. I don't recall being loaded onto a stretcher and placed into the ambulance. I have a vague memory of someone mentioning a CT scan, then nothing until I regained consciousness in the ER. Supposedly, a chest x-ray was done. Not sure what drugs they gave me, but two days later my body is still sore and I'm tired and feel like shit.

CHAPTER ELEVEN

2024—Hope

Sometimes a win doesn't mean you've crossed the finish line first, scored the winning goal, or was better than your opponent. Sometimes winning has nothing to do with anyone else, it's merely an accomplishment or goal you achieved. Scoring a win is as simple as trying something new, pushing yourself beyond your comfort zone. Or, recapturing a piece of yourself from years ago just to see if you could. A win without winning isn't a loss. Sometimes just the act of trying counts as a win. Having the courage to attempt new things, branch out and explore new horizons belongs in the win column. To be successful isn't about fame and fortune, having a big house or fancy car. Success is measured by how often you try and continue trying. Success is not giving up, letting the earth swallow you closing you off from everything.

My most recent win was attending a Stampeders game. Going to a live game for the first time in seven years. Did I make it to the end of the fourth quarter? No, I didn't. Did I stay until half time? Nope. We arrived an hour before kickoff and left after the first quarter. Was I disappointed? Yes. Upset? Not really. As my son said when we arrived home... "I'm proud of you Mom for trying." While I'm glad I tried it, and although I didn't make it to the end, I am proud of myself for not giving up.

No matter how hard the terrain is, the length of the journey, or how harsh the climate, if we never try, if we roll over and surrender never attempt anything new, we cannot change and without change we do not learn.

My philosophy is it's better to move forward than remain stagnant. So, take the next step in your journey today ignore your doubts, everyone has them from time to time, and spread your wings and embrace new things.

Journal Entry, February 4, 2024

Memory issues continue to plague me. Like the other day when getting Devon some water, I poured it, threw in some ice and then instead of giving it to him, I set it on the counter and headed to the bathroom to shower. Afterwards, he called me into the den, held up a glass and asked for water.

"What?! You want more again?! Shesh, aren't you a thirsty one!" I started to walk away when his words stopped me.

"Mom. You didn't give me any water. You were going to but..." I cut him off.

"What are you talking about? Of course I did. I even put ice in it." I looked at him, confused. Stood for a moment, brows furrowed, eyes moving back n' forth thinking, did I not give it to him? Did I get the water? Turning, I strode back into the kitchen to the fridge looked around and didn't see his glass on the counter, or the stove. Frowning, I turned towards the island, and as I did, I spied the glass sitting on the counter by the phone, filled to the rim with ice bobbing against the sides. I was sure I'd taken it to him before heading to the shower, had assumed he drank it and wanted more. But I couldn't recall getting the water let alone taking it to him. Was this just old age creeping in, or was I losing it?

Ugh. I'm getting so fed up with this! Starting something, then forgetting what I was doing. Like when I had left the hot water running, turned away to chop up some carrots while listening to music on my headphones totally unaware of the sink filling, overflowing to the next, then creeping across the island counter to the edge, cascading over like a waterfall pooling on the floor. When I realized what I'd done, I immediately turned it off and plunged each hand into a sink to pull the plugs, ignoring the pain of the scalding water on my fingers. It took every towel we owned to sop up the puddle created by my forgetfulness. Too heavy with water, we set up the drying rack in the bathtub draping the towels over each rung with fans blowing to speed up the process.

Since then, I won't listen to music while working in the kitchen just to be sure. Flooding the kitchen was a reminder that I couldn't perform more than one task at a time. Had to focus on what I was doing and not split my attention. Multi-tasking was no longer an option like it had been. Before, when I was working, I prided myself on my ability to talk and type, write notes and listen all at the same time. It was easier back then when my brain functioned normally and before the surgeries. It was an asset I could no longer boast of, could only wish for knowing it wasn't possible. And despite eating and sleeping better, exercising, and managing my moods and not overdoing things, I still have problems understanding instructions, forgetting what I was going to say or mixing up words. I can't even read calendar entries correctly, mixing up the start and end times often arriving late to appointments or missing them entirely.

Overall, my health is better. I've lost weight, am eating healthier, exercise is up and down but more up, and sleep is about the same as it has been. I've got new hearing aids which are working out well, my double vision is good, and the glaucoma is under control. The cardiologist I saw last August isn't too concerned about the abnormal ECGs and feels they're related to the seizures.

Journal Entry, March 18, 2024, Questions for Dr. Young

1. Is Cenobamate[11] an option for me?
2. What about Vimpat? Never got a chance to see if it would work because of toxicity in 2018, now on only two meds vs four, should we give it a try? I.e. remove Dilantin & replace with Vimpat?

Journal Entry, March 20, 2024, Seizure note

Confused wandered room to room not sure why. Was looking for my phone? Went to Devon's room and laid down didn't feel good. The seizure began. Twitching I think my breathing laboured. The Ativan Devon gave me helped but then the seizure started up again. I don't think I lost awareness; I can't recall.

The stressors I now faced combined with the past the ongoing seizures, anxiety, depression, inability to perform basic tasks, and the guilt of my son's-imposed role as caregiver, have contributed to the onset of FND² with seizures.

Case in point, the death of my mother. Since April 1, 2020, I've had at least one seizure in the months leading up to the anniversary of her passing; January 16 & 19 and March 29, 2021, February 28 and March 21, 2022, January 24, 2023, and March 20, 2024. Every single year my overloaded emotions explode resulting in a seizure. But again, which was FND², and which was epilepsy? We can guess or assume they're all FND² based on when they occurred, and there's always the possibility of both. It isn't unheard of to experience both a functional and epileptic seizure within the same episode making it even harder to determine which is which.

Journal Entry, April 8, 2024

Did I have a seizure? I was washing dishes. when a sudden head rush and nausea type sensation rose from my gut. Was there a smell? Maybe? It lasted less than three minutes. I remember sitting down and listening to cello. I may have dozed off. Earlier, I had some pain in the right ear, and was tired, exhausted almost. Don't know why. I had a good sleep. I thought I'd get some fresh air and go to Staples but decided not to and even cancelled my visit to the Epilepsy Association for tomorrow and will go on Thursday.

Journal Entry, April 17, 2024

It's been a busy year so far. The seizure unit, fully occupied most weeks, extended my volunteer visits beyond three hours some days. The number of patients under investigation for FND² with seizures have increased again. And, of course, I spent more time visiting with them. My own experiences with FND[2] with seizures, plus epilepsy, provides a valuable resource for these patients. And I'm happy to provide the support they need during their stay.

The Canadian Epilepsy Alliance approached me to participate in their media blitz targeting the provincial health authorities on the delay in approving a new epilepsy drug. Health Canada approved Xcopri (Cenobamate)[11] in June 2023 but the provincial authorities hadn't followed suit. This new drug could help so many people like me with refractory epilepsy (drug resistant). But the price tag attached to it is exorbitant. Without the approvals, the cost per individual could be as high as $4,000 per year. An amount far outside the reach of the average person with epilepsy. Many are unemployed, working part-time, and earning minimum wage. There isn't the extra income to cover those costs. It's so frustrating to know there's a potential medication that could control seizures for hundreds, even thousands of people but is inaccessible because of the province's delay. There shouldn't be a need to reach out to the media begging health authorities to perform their jobs in a timely manner.

I did manage to reach three months without a seizure. March 20th was the last one. I'm pretty sure it was an epileptic event. I remember the confusion, how I couldn't locate my phone, and hadn't any sense of where I was or what I was doing. Eventually I collapsed on Devon's bed. I hadn't felt well, experienced rising and nausea. Not sure but I believe Dev gave me a couple Ativan. And, as per usual, when I didn't respond, Devon called 911. There's a vague memory of being shifted, pants removed, and a sharp jab. My breathing became difficult, hadn't noticed the paramedics arrive, load me up on the stretcher, leave the apartment, down the elevator, and hadn't noticed when they loaded me up in the ambulance. I awakened in the ER unaware of how much time had passed. Whether it was the drugs they'd given me or the seizure itself, I don't have a clear memory of my visit. I have no idea if a doctor spoke to me. Don't recall any questions about missing a dose or how low my Dilantin levels were, or which type of seizure I had. Maybe these questions were asked and answered. Devon informed me afterwards the paramedics and me conversed a little as they wheeled me out of the apartment. If that was the case, I hadn't any idea of what they said or how I responded. One thing was odd about this trip, my Dilantin levels weren't checked. If they overlooked requesting it, or if the doctor covering the ER was a rookie or hadn't felt it necessary, I'll never know. It's possible they dismissed my epilepsy and focused on the FND[2] with seizures. It wouldn't be the first time doctors believed all my episodes were functional versus epileptic and I'm certain it won't be the last.

As a result of this seizure, I didn't get into the SMU the following week. I'd planned on going the Sunday, as both Monday and Tuesday were booked. Kenneth was going on Thursday and on Friday is the annual Purple Day by Night[10] Gala hosted by the Epilepsy Association of Calgary. Just as well since I wasn't sleeping well. I'd run out of my Melatonin and the quality and quantity of my sleeping pattern had gone to shit. But I didn't feel guilty. Unless a new patient was admitted to bed B, there was only one new patient to visit. Of the remaining two beds, one has passed on our visits and the other we'd both seen. So, if I don't get in this week, it won't be the end of the world.

I hope this new drug, Xcopri (Cenobamate)[11] will be an option for me. Since the province hasn't approved it yet, I'll need Dr. Young to submit a special authority request. I'll still have to pay for it myself as BlueCross won't cover it until it's approved. It's unclear if I would stay on the Dilantin. Of my two drugs, the Lamotrigine wouldn't interact as bad as the Dilantin. If this new drug is an option, I'd feel more comfortable if I was admitted to the seizure unit while adjusting my medications. The last time we tried to wean me off one med and introduce another, my liver couldn't filter out the drugs fast enough and I became toxic. (drug toxicity is like an overdose). By adjusting my meds in the unit, we could dispense with the usual weaning/titration protocols. I hope that's an option we can explore. And, who knows, maybe a visit to the SMU might help to determine if the seizures have changed. I know surgery isn't an option, but if the seizures are generating from a new location maybe there's other drugs we could try?

I've noticed the tingling sensation in my left arm hasn't been occurring as often and, in my opinion, most of my seizures are epileptic. The confusion, aura-type sensations, losing awareness, brief moments of lip twitching, the drug levels for both Dilantin and Lamotrigine have dropped, mixing up words, and memory blips have increased.

Journal Entry, May 3, 2024

I'm sick and tired of medical professionals who continue to use the outdated term pseudo seizure versus a functional seizure. Many still consider them to be an event the person can just stop. By pinching and yelling they assume it will automatically stop the event and they can go on their way. My most recent experience supported that fact.

An EMT who was obviously new concluded I was having a 'pseudo seizure' (his words) and it would subside by itself. Therefore, he downgraded the call and cancelled the firetruck which was already on its way. And despite my son informing him the correct term was a psychogenic non-epileptic seizure (PNES[1]), that I had epilepsy as well and how difficult it was to determine which type I was having, he ignored him. But when ten to fifteen minutes had passed and it hadn't subsided, he upgraded the situation, and the fire truck was dispatched again. The other EMTs who'd remained downstairs arrived just before the convulsing started. It was evident this newbie EMT was unsure of the proper protocol as he turned to his partners and asked which medication to administer. Ativan or Midazolam. Finally, after an hour from seizure onset, I was placed in the ambulance and taken to the emergency room.

Once aware of my surroundings the doctor came to speak to me. Stated it was a non-epileptic event, at least he didn't call it a pseudo seizure. He believed it wasn't epileptic because I hadn't lost consciousness. He believed that was what happened with an epileptic seizure, that someone couldn't be aware of their surroundings. Couldn't see or hear during a seizure. Regardless of which type I had, it's evident by the medical professionals I saw that day, a lack of education and understanding of either seizure type was lacking.

Journal Entry, May 31, 2024

I hadn't seen my masseuse, Beth, in over a month. I was long overdue. As usual, the right side of my neck and shoulders were hard as rock, bumpy by the knotted muscles and tendons. An issue going as far back as the early 2000s.

I could lay on that table for hours but couldn't afford to do so. An hour and a half later and back at home, body loose and moving freely. A bit of lunch, a quick nap, and onto the chores of the day. Organics, garbage, and recycling deposited in the appropriate bins, hands washed and gloved ready at the kitchen sink.

My son and I are lazy when it comes to cooking and choosing healthy options such as fruit and vegetables over processed snacks marketed as healthy alternatives. Coming from the coast where fresh produce was in abundance, the 'trucked in' fare found in grocery stores was lacking in both quality and quantity. Our fridge freezer was the standard top freezer variety offering limited space. To compensate, I purchased cases of fruit cups through Amazon, deposited five cups per container, refrigerating them for easy access.

I was in the middle of my assembly line plastic containers next to the sink, five fruit cups next to each, a strainer set in one side of the double sink, the other empty ready for empty cups and plastic lids. It's a slow task, peeling off lid—toss into empty sink—dump contents into strainer—dish into container—set aside and repeat. I hadn't gotten far along in my task when the wave hit. A rushing tide of g-force proportions rose from my stomach washing over my head. An enormous sensation disrupting my equilibrium. Lasting mere seconds, I stood there feeling like Elmer Fudd after a blow to the head, imaginary stars circling my head.

"Mom? You, okay?" came a voice from a distance. My son Devon was at my side in a moment, just in time to help me to the floor as I started to collapse. After laying me on my side, bracing me against his leg to keep me from rolling onto my back. With my eyes open, head resting on my left arm, I lay motionless, unable to speak. Coming over to my right hand, Devon held it loosely, asked if I could squeeze his hand. My fingers wouldn't respond to my brain's request, insisting on remaining still.

"Mom, can you squeeze my hand?" He asked twice over. No response. Three minutes, ten minutes—fifteen minutes later I lay there unresponsive. Although I could see and hear him, I couldn't react, my body frozen, unable to respond to the simplest request.

"Mom, this has gone on long enough, I'm calling 911." The usual questions of location, which do you need, fire or ambulance, what's happening, a brief list of questions re health conditions, and the request to remain on the line until help arrived.

The fire truck arrived first followed by an ambulance. Blood pressure, oxygen levels, eyes assessed for reaction, they examined my prone state. As the EMS took over, my legs, arms and head began shaking. Small twitches like electrical jolts jumped through nerves and muscle, steadily increasing in intensity. I could still hear and my vision was mostly intact, but the vocal cords wouldn't work.

"She's having a pseudo seizure," one said. "I don't' want to give her any benzos" said the other. She proceeded to administer the next step of assessment, painful stimuli.

Painful stimuli are exactly what the name implies. EMS will perform a sternal rub, which involves applying a firm downward pressure with the knuckles to the midsection of the patient's sternum as if using a washboard. Or, applying pain to a fingernail bed, or squeezing/pinching the trapezius.

I didn't respond to the rub down. Still hadn't spoken, and my body was still twitching. It was time to dump me on the stretcher and take me to the hospital. Unceremoniously lifted onto the stretcher and strapped in, we left the apartment. Down the elevator, out the main doors, around the corner to the waiting ambulance parked in the alley all the while shaking and jerking upon the stretcher. Once loaded and IV inserted, a second rub down administered more vigorous than the first, fingertips poked and eyes checked, we headed out. No sirens, no racing through streets it was as if we were on a Sunday drive or road trip to nowhere.

I never spoke on our way to emergency. My plight seemed inconsequential, a source of mild entertainment, or at least that's how it appeared to me.

Wheeled past triage without so much as a word, down a narrow brightly lit hallway past a line of beds tucked up against one wall to the end. We were a line of cars stuck in rush hour traffic, a row of ugly ducklings returning to the nest. Speechless and unresponsive, I lay there for all to see. No regard for my privacy. I'm not sure how long I lay there when the convulsing began once more. It started with my legs progressed to my torso, arms, and head. In rapid succession my legs shook like a swimmer kicking racing the length of the pool. So violent was the motion, it lifted my ass off the stretcher. As it increased, my upper body convulsed in tandem performing sit-ups as each leg hit the bed. With arms now flailing and head shaking, my seizure was in a full on grandmal. On and on and on it went, my body contorted. My right arm was lifted hoping for a reaction, but remained elevated when released, my hand flipping as it stayed upright as if waving to a crowd. I've no clue how long I seized. What time it was, how long ago this all started but after it stopped and my voice returned, I signalled to the EMS who brought me there.

"I want you to know your use of the term pseudo seizure is demeaning and upsetting to patients. Pseudo means fake and these seizures are real, not a put on for attention or drugs. Known as psychogenic nonepileptic seizures, or FND[2] with seizures, they're difficult to differentiate from an epileptic one.

I informed them I have both, my situation is complex and even my neurologist has told emergency doctors it's extremely difficult to tell which one I'm having." I went on to tell them my story, the three surgeries performed from 2016 – 2018, and how my epilepsy is resistant to drugs. They admitted my case was atypical and they hadn't seen anything like it before, but their confession did nothing for me felt like an excuse. And the reason for referencing them as pseudo seizures? It was easier than calling them nonepileptic, psychogenic nonepileptic, or FND[2] with seizures.

Shortly after a space opened up and I was wheeled away to a bed. Blood was eventually withdrawn and sent off for testing, a brief word from the doctor and I was left to my own defenses.

This was the first time whether epileptic or functional, that I'd seized for over an hour without any medication to relieve the situation. It was the first time my epilepsy was never addressed. It was the first time I felt such distress since I left BC. This hospital which had been my haven for over five years, was now no better than the ones I left behind. It finally hit home that my dual diagnosis wouldn't, and couldn't, receive the awareness and level of care it needed.

I was in this by myself and the only way to help myself and others like me, was to share my story and advocate for the respect and care we deserve.

Journal Entry, June 1, 2024

My longest day: the compilation of hours grouped together strung by a thread of waiting and anticipation of the moments of tiresome seconds and minutes of spatial connection which increase the anxiety and depression.

Blocks of time tick away unnoticed until that moment my body is taken over by some alien force pulling strings moving my limbs as a puppet at the whim of its master. Controlled and manipulated all thought suppressed on a course of submission no control no feelings except for my body in distress.

All I want for me what I wish to be is to have in my life some normalcy. An end to weakness and pain emergency trips ambulance rides feeling tired and abused. Feeling lonely abandoned and isolated living within my head.

What I'd like to see for others and for me is an end to this tyranny. Of doctors sympathetic to our plight to our body vs mind and this endless fight. I want peace and an end to my plight.

Live out my years without fighting this fight wanting to take flight.

Oh, if only I may see an end to this day stop the seconds, the minutes, and hours of this my ongoing mess.

Journal Entry, June 20, 2024

Started with rising escalating to confusion disorientation. Responded to Devon but quite confused, eventually becoming nonresponsive. Clonic episode followed by loss of awareness. Taken to ER, two doses of Midazolam(?) plus the one Ativan Dev gave me. I came to around 2am. Discharged at 4:30am(?) Disoriented, confused, called out to Dev, used Google home to page him as couldn't see phone to call him Dev said I was confused could respond to some degree at first then just grunts. Ativan given recall him calling 911. Then nothing.

Journal Entry, July 10, 2024, follow-up appointment with Dr. Young

I sat with the fellow and a visiting neurologist from Europe reviewing my recent spate of seizure activity and trips to the ER. We discussed my medications and my willingness to try the Cenobamate

(Xcopri)[11] and look to remove the Dilantin. After twenty minutes, they left the room to discuss our conversation and possible options with Dr. Young.

After what seemed like ages, all three returned to review their thoughts and what scenarios we could look at going forward.

" Hello, Ms. McClure, how are you doing? The last time I saw you you were quite distraught. Have things improved?" Without waiting for an answer, he continued. "You're a warrior Ms. McClure. A true warrior." His smile was genuine, his words half spoken to me and his fellows. "But you need to look after yourself. You spend so much time helping others you forget about you. While it's commendable and you do so much for the patients, you must take time to care for you and your well-being. Okay?"

"Yes. I was a bit emotional. I'm just so tired of these seizures, without knowing which is happening, the anxiety, and...and the effects on my...moods. Maybe I should get back into therapy. I've noticed since last year my moods have been slipping." Grabbing tissues from the box on the desk and dabbing at the moisture building in my eyes. Just waiting for the onslaught to follow.

"It certainly has been difficult. And as you know, the only way to know for sure is to come in to the unit. We need to figure out if these seizures you're having at home are non-epileptic or not. Once we have a clearer picture, we'll see when you can get in to see someone. What about Dr. Samson? Have you considered her?"

"No. Dr. Samson and I are more like colleagues. I mean, she doesn't want to take me on as a patient. She wants to keep our options open for any further volunteer activities down the road."

"Ah, yes that makes sense. Okay, so, is another visit into the unit something you want to do? Come back to figure this out? It probably won't be until September with the unit closing for August, which I'm sure you know." Nodding his head at me, he addressed the fellows, "She knows more about how the unit operates than I do!" Chuckling, he turned back to me, "So, Ms. McClure. What are your thoughts? Do you want to come back in?"

"Sure. why not? Might as well go in for visit number six. If we can sort this out, it'll help. The anxiety of if, when, which seizure type is occurring just increases the possibility of an event. If Dev and I can figure out which type it is, that'll help immensely." The tears overflowed requiring another dip into the tissue box. "But, what about this new medication? The Cenobamate[11]? Is it something we should look at?" Since the news of this new drug, my hopes of a miracle a life free of seizures, was a topic I couldn't dismiss, thought about constantly.

"No, it's just like all the others. Not an option as it wouldn't make much difference in your case." He stood, smiled and turned towards the door. "Okay then, we'll put in the request to bring you back into the SMU and then go from there. Enjoy your summer and take care of yourself and we'll see you soon." He left the room followed by his fellows. Gathering my belongings, I too exited the tiny office and headed out. Waiting for the elevator I started to chuckle. Sheesh. I thought my days in the SMU were over. Number six?!

SMU VISIT 2024

JULY 11, 2024—JULY 18, 2024

Journal Entry, July 12, 2024

With the seizure unit closing for the month of August, I didn't want to mess around and stayed awake all night. Sleep deprivation being one of my triggers was the quickest way to get any results. And it worked.

A vice grip type feeling encircled my head creating a woozy, lightheaded effect. I sat and stared straight ahead listening to the beeps of the monitors. The nurses arrived after I pressed the button, asked me the usual questions. Where was I? What's my name? The date? To which I couldn't respond. As usual I could see and hear but couldn't speak. I was fully aware of the blood pressure cuff being wrapped around my left arm, the pressure as it filled, and the oxygen clamp attached to my index finger. I can't recall how long it lasted but as it eased, I could speak slowly yet with some difficulty in pronouncing words. My left side was weak my blinking slow and steady.

Journal Entry, July 13, 2024

Had a great sleep slept for over eight hours! Guess I was tired. It figures! In the middle of shifting rooms, I had a seizure but wasn't connected to the system. UGH! It was the usual rising sensation head all floaty and lasted less than five minutes.

During rounds Dr. Young confirmed what I suspected, yesterday's event wasn't captured on EEG and the consensus was a functional seizure. The game plan is to remain on my current medications and dosages and see if the EEG registers any activity. We already know if we remove my meds, I will have epileptic seizures. What we want to see is what occurs during the ones I have at home. And I'm to sleep deprive again tonight.

Journal Entry, July 14, 2014

Why the increase in seizures this year? Are they all functional ones? So far, in here, in the SMU, they're the clonic events without any EEG correlation. I should be relieved. I should be happy no epileptic seizures have been captured, that they're all functional and, yet I feel somewhat disappointed. Why? Where's the reasoning behind that? Am I nuts?

I'm so relieved we weren't reducing my meds. While *I'm n ot o n~~the ~ falling~~ of?   wa~ `tr~~`` isng?*
Man I'm`~~ tred~ ~~ could sle~`p of `~`~~~g ee n g

In some weird way, I'm almost thankful they're not but then, are they *all* functional seizures? Has my epilepsy been halted by the surgeries? Should I remain on my meds if I'm not having epileptic events? I don't know....*sigh...*

Journal Entry, July 15, 2014

Still not seeing anything on the EEG but that doesn't mean I don't have epilepsy.

"Ms. McClure, there's an analogy I use in these situations which I'd like to share, if I may?"

I looked at him with interest, nodding my head in response to his question. He settled further into the folding chair, readying himself to impart his wisdom.

Tears blurred my vision slightly. I twisted my fingers around the sheet trying hard not to cry like I did in his office last week. "I felt... I thought by helping others... I could... I... can... forget about... ...my issues." He nodded understanding.

"Think of epilepsy like a frozen lake. When it's 'active' in the early days the ice was 'thin'. Now, after your surgeries and the passage of time, it's getting thicker. Do you understand?" He'd sat forward as he spoke, elbows on knees, speaking slowly and clearly.

"So...what you're saying is...because I'm not having many epileptic seizures...and...whether the medication or surgeries have helped...or not...my seizure threshold has increased? Is that what you mean?" My eyes were focused on my lap as I spoke not wanting to be distracted as I chose my words only raising them to his after I'd finished.

"Yes, exactly! Smiling he sat back and crossed his legs, resuming his relaxed position on the uncomfortable chair. "So, now, we will keep your meds the same. The reasons being:

You're not experiencing any adverse side effects at present and if they're controlling the epileptic events why change things and there's no point weaning off while here to get a comparison, because we already know with less medication you'll have seizures.

In about 15% of cases, if we stop your meds and if epileptic seizures resurface, as this can happen, it's harder to get back to the same level of control. And remember...having a long seizure doesn't necessarily mean its epilepsy. Which brings me to you going to the emergency. There isn't any point in calling 911 and going to the hospital because, what are they going to do? They'll pump you up with Ativan, Midazolam, and possibly Dilantin, run some bloodwork, monitor you, then send you home. It's better you do not call them unless you're badly injured, of course. You know what I'm saying?"

"No. I mean, yes, I understand. But the Ativan isn't working anymore even at two doses. And the seizures are going on for forty-five minutes or more before Devon calls and most times the paramedics administer at least one dose of Midazolam, if not two. Devon can't just stand there and watch me seize for an hour or more and not do *anything*!" Tears were beginning to trickle down my cheeks as the memory of May's seizures came flooding back.

"It's possible you've become used to the Ativan therefore reducing its efficacy. We will look to changing up your rescue medication to avoid these trips to the hospital. Maybe Midazolam would work best. The Ativan works slower than Midazolam, and the Midazolam will make you drowsy and probably put you to sleep."

"Would Devon have to inject it? Like what the paramedics do? Like jab it into my leg or something?"

"No. No. It'll be a syringe that he fills and squirts into your mouth between the cheek and gums. No needles." At this he rose, indicating to the fellow, nurse, and technologist who were standing quietly inside the door listening to our exchange, it was time to leave. "Okay, Ms. McClure, we'll continue to get as much information on the EEG and capture as many events as possible so we can get you home."

"Okay. But can I quickly ask one question?" Turning, he nodded for me to proceed. "What about the long-term effects of the Dilantin on my liver and bones? And, what about the Lamotrigine? Shouldn't we be concerned about this?"

Leaning on the footrail Dr. Young shook his head, "No. We're not that worried about this. Dilantin is a good medication, and we're not too concerned about the effects on the liver short-term, however, we do need to monitor the effect on your bones. The Lamotrigine has no real side effects in comparison to Dilantin. The only things to watch for with Lamotrigine is tingly fingers and toes. And rest assured, Ms. McClure, if down the road there's any concerns, we would address them. Okay?" He smiled and spying the uneaten hardboiled egg on my breakfast tray, asked "Are you going to eat that?" He made to grab it as he spoke.

"Yes! I am!" I snatched it up, "This is my one guilty pleasure while I'm in here and you can't have it!" I laughed as he raised his arms in surrender and scurried out the door, chuckling.

After they left, I read over my notes, closed my eyes, leaned back against the pillows.

'Dr. Young makes sense. My epilepsy, while not 100% controlled, is manageable more so than before. And while I may still be having some seizures, they're not as prevalent as the functional ones. He said it's possible for FND² with seizures to mimic or adopt similar features of my epileptic ones which, again, makes sense. I guess over time, my brain has incorporated them within my "software" and the "coding" has been rewritten to include my "waves", confusion, losing awareness, and left sided weakness. These combined with paralysis, hearing and seeing, the inability to speak or respond in any way, plus the shaking have become my so-called functional seizures. Even the gobbledegook I'd written yesterday has been assimilated. This jibber jabber hasn't happened in years, maybe even before the first surgery. When I showed it to Dr. Young, he found it quite interesting. Not sure if it was something new to him, or if it was just something I hadn't shown him before.'

Journal Entry, July 17, 2024

Another seizure this morning, most likely a functional one as it lasted for over an hour. Very similar to both the May 31ˢᵗ and June 20ᵗʰ events. Had some rising, was lightheaded, staring, dopey feeling, then escalated into a tonic clonic. Extreme tiredness, weak and sore limbs, so bad it takes great effort to move them. This was much like the ones last year in June and December with the addition of the inability to respond. There seems to be a pattern here.

- staring
- unresponsive after a period
- head pressure
- hearing and seeing intact, but cannot speak
- body paralyzed, can't lift legs or move hands
- escalates to tonic clonic in varying degrees

I'm still tired after three hours. My body is moving slow as is my brain. I'm at five days now in the unit, have deprived myself of sleep on three of the nights, and had three or four seizures. Of course, this morning's event occurred just as Dr. Young was starting rounds. I assume we'll just carry on and see how many more events occur. Eli, the nurse on duty, confirmed she witnessed my seizure earlier. I think that's the first time she's seen one "live". She wants me to stay awake again tonight. I guess every other night is working even though none are epileptic. But that's okay. It's a good thing. The more info they get the easier it will be to understand what's going on and come up with a plan.

Journal Entry, July 18, 2024

Dr. Young and his crew squeezed into my room with the day's update. It was apparent that all four events captured during my stay were FND[2] with seizures. We will keep my medications the same. A prescription for Midazolam will be written and a referral placed for therapy with the neuropsychologist, most likely Dr. Jenny who's back from maternity leave! Yay!

I'm to let Devon know if the Midazolam doesn't work and if he believes I'm having an epileptic event, he is to call 911.

Note:
    - my epileptic seizures wouldn't include shaking
    - I would lose awareness
    - I wouldn't be able to hear or see during the seizure (e.g. the event in the elevator at Foothills).

"As far as I'm concerned Ms. McClure, you can go home today or wait until tomorrow. We've got all that we need and once we've reviewed everything, my office will contact you to arrange a follow-up appointment. Thanks for coming in. It's good that we now know which type you're having at home. And with some additional therapy, who knows, maybe you'll gain some control over the functional seizures. You take care of yourself and have a great summer!" The room felt like an empty cavern after they'd gone. It was my sixth visit, and I was back in the room where the topic of non-epileptic seizures was first discussed. Kinda feels like I've come full circle.

Journal Entry, August 16, 2024

The month's half over and I feel like I've accomplished absolutely nothing. Discharged from the SMU almost a month ago and I should be happy, or at least happier. Knowing the seizures haven't been epileptic should be comforting but the anxiety is still there to some degree. I don't think that'll ever go away entirely.

The referrals to both the neuropsychologist in the epilepsy clinic and the therapists the kind lady at Alberta Mental Health recommended were placed and I've already heard back from both. Dr. Jenny is back from maternity leave, so I'll get to see her again on August 29th! Yippee! I really like her. Seems fitting she was the last one I saw at the clinic and who I'll be seeing now. I received an email the other day from the therapist's office with instructions to set up an account and complete intake forms. The sessions will be done virtually and are free. Alberta Mental Health had provided a few options, some free and others pay for service, but I opted to go with free. My first session is booked for August 20th, my birthday. Maybe that's a good omen. The rebirth of a new and improved Linda. I think I'll go with that!

For the first time I feel hopeful about the future. Certain pieces are falling into place. Devon finished his schooling, has a great job that he loves, and his life is finally moving forward. And I've grown too. Although there's been an increase in seizure activity and I returned to the SMU, I've learned a lot about myself and my seizures. I have answers to questions I thought couldn't be solved. We have a new plan and how to implement it. The rescue medication has been updated, my seizure medications remain unchanged, and I'm back in therapy. We set up Lifeline[16] back in June. I wear a pendant now whether I'm out or at home. It has GPS that works off cellular networks allowing ambulances and paramedics to locate me should I need assistance. We even have a lockbox on our apartment door so they can get in when I'm alone and I can call for help with the press of a button. It's taken me a bit to accept the need for such a device, but the benefits do outweigh the alternatives. I appease myself knowing it reduces Devon's anxiety over leaving me at home for hours at a time; do not want a repeat of March 15, 2015, and my three hour seiz-a-thon.

While it's been a wild ride the last nine years and we've hit many a pothole, or five, I can't say it hasn't been a learning experience. I know way more about how the brain functions than I ever learned in high school. Had more surgical procedures and tests than the average household. My taste in music now includes Mozart and classical cello, I'm reading nonfiction just as much as fiction. I follow medical journals, subscribe to newsletters, follow associations devoted to epilepsy and functional neurological disorders on Facebook and LinkedIn. My volunteer activities include epilepsy associations, hospitals, and international groups whose purpose is to support those with epilepsy. I'm an author, a poet, and sometime media spokesperson. My brain has been cracked open three times and has twenty-eight holes drilled into it.

I have double vision, glaucoma, elevated cholesterol and liver panels, arthritis, and some cognitive dysfunctions. But all of that hasn't stopped me. I'm stubborn and ornery to the core. And there's a reason I'm like that, a purpose for what I've been through, and a reason for writing *Battles of The Mind* and now *Mind Games*.

The purpose is to share. The reason? Because it helps people. And the reason it's happening now? It was meant to.

We may not have control of many things, if any, but of those we can steer in the right direction, why shouldn't we get behind the wheel and drive? I've always liked to help others and if I have the ability and willingness to support others, then why wouldn't I?

FINAL THOUGHTS

What we need is...

What we need is a brighter future for those who have nowhere to turn. Whether they have FND² or both epilepsy and FND², there's a gap in the system these unfortunate individuals slip through. Associations designed to help those with epilepsy and/or mental health issues either don't have the expertise or government funding to offer programs aimed at treating FND². Only a handful of psychologists and psychiatrists know of or have training to support their patients with FND². Group sessions may not provide the right setting for some and could trigger their seizures. What then can you offer patients who have seizure disorders other than epilepsy? One-on-one counselling with professionals versed in therapies designed to address the trauma, emotional stress, anxieties, and depression is one component. What is missing is the connection to a community of like-minded individuals with lived experience. Only another patient with FND² can fully understand the frustrations, anxiety, depression, stigma, and false accusations of faking it, the assumption the seizures aren't real and are triggered at will. A person with FND² face the same discriminations as a person with epilepsy. And a person with both epilepsy and FND² are affected two-fold.

What we need is peer-to-peer support. A network of patients matched with another sharing similar experiences. Expanding their network of support to include a mentor will not only reduce the sense of isolation and loneliness, but also foster a community where no one feels alone. With resources for mental health being as limited as they are, offering a means to support one another through the lived experiences of others seems to be the best, and right, option.

One Last Message

The brain, much like a symphony orchestra, must work in concert. If just one instrument is out of tune, the synchronicity is disrupted, creating a cacophony.

Trauma doesn't necessarily refer to abuse, such as physical or mental attacks from without. Trauma can be experienced in any moment, hopefully not for years, where the brain cannot handle the situation.

We learn from repetition. From the moment of our birth, we begin a journey of constant learning, gaining knowledge as we become familiar with our surroundings. With each milestone, we store this new information for future reference, adding to it with each subsequent mile marker. As we travel through life, we return to those experiences using the data as a guide. Just like a researcher or scientist, we cross-reference each data point against the current problem, hoping to find the right equation to solve the question. Referring to our experiences and how we dealt with them previously is a natural process. Unfortunately, sometimes those experiences and their negative results can follow us into a vicious circle of repetition. In addition, our memories are not exact replicas of what transpired and can alter after time. Without a detailed accounting, the information we retrieve may not provide the full story. If those experiences we're stuck in are a misrepresentation of the facts, are exaggerated or faulty, our reactions to similar events may repeat themselves in the future. In other words, our fight or flight mode remains engaged, recreating the same scenarios over and over.

Strictly speaking from lived experience, and from the articles, podcasts, and books I've read and listened to, retraining my brain, that is, the thought processes, is key to managing my functional seizures. The overthinking, jumping to conclusions, the knee-jerk negative responses, being a mind reader, psychic, time traveler, and all-round pessimist, must stop. By embracing the principles of Cognitive Behaviour Therapy (CBT) and incorporating mindfulness techniques, and keeping an open mind, will increase the control I have over my seizures.

All it takes is awareness…Being in touch with the senses of body and mind…Focusing on the sensations of life, without judgement…Reaching within and experiencing the moment…Forgetting all preconceived ideations of what is and what isn't…Opening the mind to the possibilities of now, not tomorrow…Closing the mind to the negative influences of the past, shutting the door, and locking it... Breathe in the cool fresh air, releasing the stale hot air of negativity hiding within…experience each day in spaces of time, as pieces of a puzzle without pictures just waiting to be created.

Since I moved to Calgary, I've met others with functional seizures whose stories are a lot like those I've read about.

"My doctors thought I was crazy."

"I thought I was going crazy."

"My father doesn't believe me. He says I'm faking my seizures to get attention."

"I've been in and out of hospital so often, I'm afraid to go there. It's a safe place, but I'm not comfortable there."

"I feel bad that my mom must step in and look after my son. We were doing fine until the seizures started."

"I want a normal life."

"My sons are old enough to understand, but I hate the thought of what my seizures are doing to them and what they feel when they see me having one."

"My eight-year-old doesn't understand. He tells me afterwards, 'mommy had a panic attack,' and he shakes to show me what he saw."

And the common thread of *Guilt—Fear—Shame; Sad—Lonely—Hopeless* are the same whether you're twenty-four or forty.

I've experienced those same emotions and more. Past trauma, COVID, feeling unworthy, needing help and the inability to ask for it. Losing a life that was and left with a present and future full of fear and loneliness. The stress, isolation, death, and illness during COVID was the perfect setting for the FND[2] with seizures to develop.

I've never felt so alone since my functional seizure diagnosis. Although I eventually connected with others who had epilepsy, I can't say the same for having both. It's difficult to carry on each day without another who can relate. Exposed to health professionals not versed in the mechanics of a functional neurological disorder and assuming they're all fake, creates a barrier to treatment which has the potential to eliminate them. Dealing with the stigma of a misunderstood condition and finding my place within neurology and psychology, is a challenge not common with epilepsy. I've devoted the last five years to arm myself with knowledge, learn from experts in the field and convey information to others like me and their families.

By sharing my story, the challenges, triumphs, and failures with those with both and others with functional seizures, I hope to offer a safe space to share and provide hope for a seizure free future.

NOTE TO READER:

Since its earliest days, functional neurological disorder (FND²) has gone through several name changes, the earliest being hysteria. Names such as psychogenic non-epileptic seizures (PNES¹²), dissociative seizures, psychogenic non-epileptic attacks (PNEA¹²), psychological non-epileptic events (PNES¹²), pseudo seizures, and non-epileptic seizures (NES¹²). In the epilepsy world FND² is referenced as psychogenic non-epileptic seizures (PNES¹²) whereas in psychiatry the current moniker is Functional Neurological Disorder with seizures and, for the purposes of this book, functional seizures, (FND²), and FND² with seizures. Regardless of what name is used, there's still the same stigma and lack of awareness attached to a condition rarely spoken of and researched even less so.

Even in today's tech savvy and highly educated world, the public, including some medical professionals, still believe FND² with seizures aren't real, are a means of gaining attention, and can be stopped and started at will. The use of the term psychogenic has in some ways fed into the belief that these episodes aren't real, leaving the patient to feel discriminated, degraded, ashamed, and alone.

As recently as 2021 a consortium comprised of American Epilepsy Society's PNES special interest group, the Functional Neurological Disorders Society, (FNDS), and members of the ILAE held several sessions debating the continued use of the term psychogenic non-epileptic seizures[12]. Through these discussions and based on input from doctors and patients, the consensus was not so much just the name, although it does play an important role, but how the diagnosis is presented to the patient.

Since November 2017 and right up to my diagnosis in September 2019, psychogenic non-epileptic seizures (PNES[1]) were the term both my doctors and I used. Knowing what I know today, and how it feels to hear "you're having a pseudo seizure" and the flippant attitude attached to those comments, I want to include the current terms in use today. And to that end, I deferred to some of the experts I often go to about all things seizure related. My question to them was: When diagnosing a patient with non-epileptic seizures, which term are you using?

[The official DSM5 (Diagnostic and Statistical Manual of Mental Disorders, fifth edition) most recent nomenclature is "Functional neurological disorder with seizures" often abbreviated to "functional seizures". The ILAE task force on functional disorders is also adopting this nomenclature. The main issue many epileptologists have is with the word "seizure" because there is a strong view that this word should be reserved for Epileptic Seizures, and instead use "event" or "attack" for functional episodes. In summary: the new official name is "Functional neurological disorder with seizures" often abbreviated to "functional seizures".]

Dr. Samuel Wiebe MD, MSc, FCAHS, FRCPC Professor of Neurology Director, Calgary Adult Epilepsy Programme, Director, Clinical Research Unit, Cumming School of Medicine, University of Calgary.

[Nowadays, we tend not to use the term PNES[1] as the word "psychogenic" has negative connotations to some. The trend is now to include the term "functional" in place of psychogenic. Given this, I use the term "functional seizure" for a convulsive event and "functional event" for events that do not involve frank convulsions (e.g., staring episodes). One term I really like that is not widely used, but used by some, is "non-epileptic attack disorder" or NEAD[12]. I have not used it yet, but I hope this term will become more popular as I think this captures different types that patients may have.]

Dr. Paolo Federico MD, PhD, FRCPC, Professor of Neurology, Epilepsy

[In the epilepsy world, FND[2] is typically referred to as psychogenic non-epileptic seizures (see LaFrance and Myers work - they both use this term I believe). In the psychiatry world, the DSM-5 (Diagnostic and Statistical Manual of Mental Disorders, fifth edition) would label them under Functional Neurological Disorder with Attacks or Seizures. This is the formal psychiatric diagnostic label. We are using this more and more in our practices because there is much more work on FND[2] in general now—attacks/seizures just being one of many forms of FND[2] out there. Websites like FND Hope and the newer (last five years) international organization on FND[2] are really providing more rationale for using FND[2] as the nomenclature of choice—but it has not really changed in the epilepsy world at this point.]

Dr. S. D. Macrodimitris (she/her), Ph.D., R. Psych., Calgary Epilepsy Programme, Department of Clinical Neurosciences, Foothills Medical Centre, Adjunct Assistant Professor, Faculty of Medicine, University of Calgary.

DEFINITIONS

Project UPLIFT[7]

Using
Practice and
Learning to
Increase
Favorable
Thoughts

Program Snapshot: Teaching participants the skills for managing and improving their mental health and quality of life.

Key Components: Increases knowledge and skills, reduces depression, and improves quality of life. Methods taught include challenging thoughts, behavioral activation, coping, problem-solving, and mindfulness. Validated mental health measures are used to screen for eligibility for the program, and other measures are used throughout the program to monitor change in mental health.

Note: *While they designed UPLIFT[7] for those living with epilepsy, I have found it helpful to manage my FND[2], in addition to my epilepsy. I*

*will even go so far to say, this program could be used for those with FND²,
with the odd tweak or two, but the medical experts haven't gotten that far
in offering a revised version.*

*I've heard that group settings for those with FND² are not
necessarily the best for participants and I understand that. Hopefully in
the future, a program is designed for those with FND². I know for me if I
knew of such an offering, it would be something to work towards. It would
provide the incentive to work diligently with my health team to manage
my FND² and reach the next step in my 'therapy,' a resource to learn and
share with others like me and add another implement to my toolbox.*

Alexithymia:[13] Difficulty in recognizing and/or verbalizing emotional experiences.

Functional Neurological Disorder:[2] Functional Neurological Disorder (FND²) is an issue of the nervous system and how the brain and body send and receive signals. It's often likened to a software problem versus hardware.

*[For example, my FND² stems from my body's inability to manage
emotional stress and when it becomes overwhelmed, it reacts physically.
My body and mind become disjointed and respond like a malfunctioning
pinball machine.]*

PNES[1]**:** Psychogenic nonepileptic seizures (PNES) are sudden, involuntary short changes in behavior, movement, a sensation and possibly awareness. PNES is an automatic reflex type reaction to a distressing situation detected by the brain. It can be either physical or an emotional response to an occurrence.

[Sometimes I can predict an oncoming functional seizure based on current events that would trigger an event. However, there are times when I do not realize I'm stressed or anxious and will be caught off guard. I have learned this will typically happen after an accumulation of emotionally charged events which unbeknownst to me, have overloaded my senses to the point where the only release comes from a seizure.]

Video Telemetry [VEEG]:[14] A video EEG (electroencephalograph) records what you are doing or experiencing on video tape while an EEG test records your brainwaves. The purpose is to be able to see what is happening when you have a seizure or event and compare the picture to what the EEG records at the same time. Sounds that occur during the testing are also recorded – this can pick up if a person talks or makes sounds during an event. By doing this, doctors reading the EEG can tell if the seizure or event was related to the electrical activity in the brain.

Status Epilepticus:[15] Status Epilepticus is when a seizure lasts longer than thirty minutes or stops and starts repeatedly without regaining a normal level of awareness and is considered a medical emergency.

SUDEP:[15] Sudden Unexplained Death in Epilepsy or SUDEP refers to the sudden death of a person with epilepsy without any determinable cause. i.e. typically, an otherwise healthy person with epilepsy suddenly dies, unobserved, while in bed. In many ways,

SUDEP is reminiscent of Sudden Infant Death Syndrome (SIDS) in newborns.

WEBSITES

The following are my ever-growing list of websites I've found in my need to understand and validate my medical conditions. Known as the 'answer girl' by old colleagues, I'm like a bulldog at the opposite end of a juicy bone. No matter how long it takes, the urge, and driving need, to learn, and dissect details is as much a part of me as my DNA. You can't have one without the other. I hope this exhaustive list provides the knowledge, understanding, and comfort it has given me as I continue to grasp the changes within me, altering the course of my life and a grudging acceptance of who, and what, I've become.

https://www.nonepilepticseizures.com/

https://fndhope.org/about-fnd-hope/

https://www.epilepsy.com/article/2014/3/truth-about-psychogenic-nonepileptic-seizures

https://www.ilae.org/news-and-media/clinical-research/mortality-in-patients-with-psychogenic-nonepileptic-seizures

https://www.neurosymptoms.org/not-imagined/4594358022

https://www.canadianepilepsyalliance.org/

https://www.canadianepilepsyalliance.org/about-epilepsy-epilepsy-safety/sudep/

https://epilepsycalgary.com/

https://www.epilepsysociety.org.uk/non-epileptic-seizures

https://sites.google.com/sheffield.ac.uk/non-epileptic-attacks/home?authuser=0

https://www.epilepsy.com/living-epilepsy/seizure-first-aid-and-safety

https://managingepilepsywell.org/uplift

https://www.ncbi.nlm.nih.gov/pmc/articles/PMC5862101/

https://cumming.ucalgary.ca/departments/dcns/programs/the-calgary-comprehensive-epilepsy-program

https://www.psychologytoday.com/ca/therapy-types/mindfulness-based-cognitive-therapy

RESOURCES

INTRODUCTION
[2]https://www.fndprogram.ca/what-functional-neurological-disorder-fnd

DISCLAIMER
[2]https://www.fndprogram.ca/what-functional-neurological-disorder-fnd

CHAPTER ONE
[2]https://www.fndprogram.ca/what-functional-neurological-disorder-fnd

CHAPTER TWO
[1]https://nonepilepticseizures.com/
https://www.fndprogram.ca/what-functional-neurological-disorder-fnd
[3]https://onlinelibrary.wiley.com/doi/pdf/10.1111/epi.14542

CHAPTER THREE
[2]https://www.fndprogram.ca/what-functional-neurological-disorder-fnd
[4] https://health.umms.org/2022/06/08/trauma-response/
[5]https://www.sheffield.ac.uk/smph/people/neuroscience/markus-reuber

[6]https://www.epilepsygroup.com/doctor16/neuropsychologists-new-york/lorna-myers-phd.htm

CHAPTER FOUR

[2]https://www.fndprogram.ca/what-functional-neurological-disorder-fnd

CHAPTER FIVE

[2]https://www.fndprogram.ca/what-functional-neurological-disorder-fnd

[7] https://managingepilepsywell.org/uplift

CHAPTER SIX

[2]https://www.fndprogram.ca/what-functional-neurological-disorder-fnd

CHAPTER SEVEN

[2]https://www.fndprogram.ca/what-functional-neurological-disorder-fnd

[7] https://managingepilepsywell.org/uplift

CHAPTER EIGHT

[1]https://nonepilepticseizures.com/

[2]https://www.fndprogram.ca/what-functional-neurological-disorder-fnd

[7] https://managingepilepsywell.org/uplift

CHAPTER NINE

[2]https://www.fndprogram.ca/what-functional-neurological-disorder-fnd

[7] https://managingepilepsywell.org/uplift

[8]https://calgary.ctvnews.ca/volunteers-offer-critical-support-and-hope-to-patients-at-calgary-s-seizure-monitoring-unit-1.6366818

[9]https://www.google.com/search?client=firefox-b-d&q=International+purple+day

CHAPTER TEN

[1]https://nonepilepticseizures.com/

[2]https://www.fndprogram.ca/what-functional-neurological-disorder-fnd

[7] https://managingepilepsywell.org/uplift

[10]https://epilepsycalgary.com/

CHAPTER ELEVEN

[1]https://nonepilepticseizures.com/

[2]https://www.fndprogram.ca/what-functional-neurological-disorder-fnd

[10]https://epilepsycalgary.com/

[11]https://calgaryherald.com/news/local-news/better-access-life-changing-epilepsy-treatments

[11]https://calgary.ctvnews.ca/step-up-and-approve-this-medication-albertans-with-epilepsy-want-access-to-xcopri-1.6742665

[11]https://www.healthing.ca/diseases-and-conditions/epilepsy/opinion-timely-access-to-promising-epilepsy-therapy-and-support-is-crucial

[11]https://www.linkedin.com/posts/laura-dickson-mba-41221529_step-up-and-approve-this-medication-albertans-activity-7156700857219043328-KoiU

[16]https://www.lifeline.ca/en/

FINAL THOUGHTS

[2]https://www.fndprogram.ca/what-functional-neurological-disorder-fnd

ONE LAST MESSAGE

[2]https://www.fndprogram.ca/what-functional-neurological-disorder-fnd

NOTE TO READER

[1]https://nonepilepticseizures.com/

[2]https://www.fndprogram.ca/what-functional-neurological-disorder-fnd

[12]https://www.ilae.org/journals/epigraph/epigraph-vol-23-issue-2-spring-2021/by-any-other-name-what-to-call-psychogenic-non-epileptic-seizures

DEFINITIONS

[1]https://nonepilepticseizures.com/

[2]https://www.fndprogram.ca/what-functional-neurological-disorder-fnd

[7] https://managingepilepsywell.org/uplift

[13]https://www.ncbi.nlm.nih.gov/pmc/articles/PMC8456171/

[14]https://www.ilae.org/journals/epigraph/epigraph-vol-21-issue-2-spring-2019/inside-the-world-of-psychogenic-seizures-diagnosis-treatment-and-stigma

[15]https://www.canadianepilepsyalliance.org

BIBLIOGRAPHY

[1]https://nonepilepticseizures.com/

[2]https://www.fndprogram.ca/what-functional-neurological-disorder-fnd

EMOTION JOURNAL

[7] https://managingepilepsywell.org/uplift

ABOUT THE AUTHOR

[7] https://managingepilepsywell.org/uplift

[8] https://calgary.ctvnews.ca/volunteers-offer-critical-support-and-hope-to-patients-at-calgary-s-seizure-monitoring-unit-1.6366818

OTHER RESOURCES

https://www.ncbi.nlm.nih.gov/pmc/articles/PMC4657778/

https://www.ilae.org/journals/epigraph/epigraph-vol-21-issue-1-winter-2019/unraveling-the-mystery-of-psychogenic-non-epileptic-seizures

BIBLIOGRAPHY

Functional Neurological Disorder—FND[2]

1. In Our Words[2], by Mary Martiros, M.Ed., and Lorna Myers, Ph.D.

2. In Our Words[2], by Markus Reuber, Gregg Rawlings, and Steven C. Schachter

3. FND Stories: Personal and Professional Experiences of Functional Neurological Disorder[2], by Markus Reuber (Editor), Maxanne McCormick (Editor), Gregg H. Rawlings (Editor), Jon Stone (Editor)

4. Psychogenic Non-Epileptic Seizure: A Guide,[1] by Lorna Myers, Ph.D.

5. The Psychogenic Non-Epileptic Seizures Pocketbook: also known as Conversion disorder with seizures Dissociative seizures Functional seizures Functional dissociative seizures Nonepileptic attack disorder[1], by Julia Doss, Lorna Myers

6. View From The Floor, by Kate Berger

7. The Color of Seizures: Living with PNES[1], by Kate Taylor and Jeffrey Underwood (RN)

8. Lowering the Shield – Overcoming Psychogenic nonepileptic seizures[1], by John Dougherty

Epilepsy

1. Epilepsy Explained: a book for people who want to know more, by Drs. Markus Reuber, Steven C. Schachter, Christian E. Elger, and Ulrich Altrup

2. Seized/Temporal Lobe Epilepsy As a Medical, Historical, and Artistic Phenomenon, by Eve LaPlante

3. Patient HM: A Story of Memory, Madness, and Family Secrets, by Luke Dittrich (grandson to the surgeon who operated on patient HM)

4. A Mind Unraveled, A True Story of Disease, Love, and Triumph, by Kurt Eichenwald

5. Beyond My Control: One Man's Struggle with Epilepsy, Seizure Surgery & Beyond, by Stuart Ross McCallum

6. Surviving Wonderland Living with Temporal Lobe Epilepsy, by Sharon R. Powell

7. Web was Woven: Epilepsy and Depression, by Sonny Chase

8. Unashamed and Unafraid, by Allison Hegedus

9. I Hate This Feeling, A Memoir of Epilepsy, Brain Surgery & Seizure Freedom, by Joe Rodriguez

Others

1. Living Like You Mean It, Use the Wisdom, and Power of your Emotions to get the Life you Really Want, by Ronald J. Frederick, Ph.D.

2. The Body Keeps the Score: Brain, Mind, and Body in the Healing of Trauma, by Bessel van der Kolk, MD.

3. When the Body Says No: The Cost of Hidden Stress, by Gabor Mate, MD.

4. The Myth of Normal: Trauma, Illness and Healing in a Toxic Culture, by

Gabor Maté MD (Author), Daniel Maté

5. Remember, The Science Of Memory And The Art Of Forgetting, by Lisa Genova

6. So-Called Normal: A Memoir of Family, Depression And Resilience, by Mark Henick

7. What Happened To You, by Oprah Winfrey and Dr. Bruce D. Perry

AWARENESS EXERCISE

(What is the body's response to emotions? How does it feel?)

1. Anger – tension, breathing shallow slightly quicker.
2. Sadness – eyes burn become moist but no tears, body deflates.
3. Happy – smile, taking deeper breaths.
4. Love – numb, body feels heavy.
5. Fear – heart rate increases, butterflies in gut, body tingly all over.
6. Guilt/shame – eyes getting moist, deflated feeling, heavy weight in gut.

EMOTION JOURNAL

(Purpose: Tracking of events to determine the when and where, accompanying feelings, and thoughts, and to identify the cause, i.e. stressors) E.g.

Date: June 16, 2020

Where: on a zoom writing session in my room.

What: rising not queasy, not lightheaded or any pressure.

Thinking: discussion about writing memoir.

Feeling: tired (only 6 -6 ½ hours of sleep) practiced grounding exercises worried about having a seizure on zoom, nervous.

Stressed: anxious about *UPLIFT*[7] session, goes back to feelings of inadequacy, and the Home Depot order still not delivered.

ABOUT THE AUTHOR

Linda grew up in Surrey, BC. Her career in the financial services industry from 1985 to 2015 abruptly ended with her epilepsy diagnosis. A single parent, she pulled up stakes and left her hometown of over fifty years to get the care she needed.

Her first memoir, Battles of The Mind was published January 2023 on Amazon and Audibles and is now available on Kobo. Her story has reached households in Canada, US, UK, Brazil, and Australia benefiting those looking for support and understanding. Her love of poetry began in her teens, developing into journaling, and her memoirs. Her poetry, written under her pen name Anne Paterson, has appeared in Riverbabble, Medium.com, the 2019, 2020, 2021, 2022, and 2023 Poetry Marathon Anthologies, and Issue #9 of Wishbone Words.

Linda volunteers at Foothills Medical Centre in their Peer-to-Peer[8] Support Program in the Seizure Monitoring Unit, is a Peer Mentor and co-facilitator for the UPLIFT[7] and PACES programs offered through the Epilepsy Association of Calgary, and a Community Council member with the International Bureau for Epilepsy.

She currently lives in Calgary with her son, Devon, and their cat, Coco.

WHAT DO I MEAN BY MINDFULNESS?

It's the sense of calm that comes with being in tune with your body, feeling the heartbeat, and the blood flow. Escaping within yourself, insulating against the surrounding noise. Breathing deeply, in, out, in, out, taking in the fresh oxygen and expelling the air of negativity from within a tensed body, stressed by life. Learning the mechanics of the physical in relation to the brain, a complex organ of muscle, veins, and electrical energy which surges through minute wires powering organs, limbs, fingers, and toes. Engaging the fluid movement of an inner being which ebbs and flows like the gentle lapping of water washing over rocks and shells caressing the shoreline.

Mindfulness lifts the spirit, allowing it to soar above the clouds, releasing the polluted air of despair. Mindfulness releases negativity and opens the mind, making room for a peaceful moment.

www.ingramcontent.com/pod-product-compliance
Lightning Source LLC
Chambersburg PA
CBHW022112040426
42450CB00006B/670